Caregiver

My Tempestuous Journey

To: Charie

God gives us love to pass on to others – that's what caregivers do.
Thanks for all you do

In Christ

Glen A. Hinshaw

John 13:35

Glen A. Hinshaw

Caregiver
My Tempestuous Journey

Author: Glen A. Hinshaw

Publisher: Glen A. Hinshaw

Cover photo taken by the author near the Lizard Head Wilderness in the San Juan National Forest

Copyright 2015 © Glen A. Hinshaw

Printed by Createspace.com
Available through Amazon.com and local booksellers

ISBN 13: 978-1517653811

1 Caregiver, 2, Aging, 3 Alzheimer's, 4 Dementia, 5 Grief

TABLE OF CONTENTS

I DEDICATE THIS BOOK

To my family and extended family who have supported me throughout this journey.

To professional and home caregivers who lovingly look after those afflicted with dementia, Alzheimer's diseases and other maladies.

To the staff of the Senior Community Care Center, Montrose, Colorado [PACE]

To the administration and staff at Valley Manor Care Center in Montrose, Colorado who cared for my mother, wife, and me.

To Region 10 for connecting caregivers with the resources they need to meet the needs of their loved ones.

To caregiver support groups that encourage others on their journey.

To the deacons and congregation of Montrose Presbyterian Church

ACKNOWLEDGEMENTS

I wish to acknowledge the following people for their contributions to this book:

John Fitzmaurice, Mark Hunzaker, Arlene Hinshaw Johnson, Laird Landon Jr. PhD, Beth Short, Will and Betty Wyatt,

I especially acknowledge George Harpole and Bob Scott for their many hours of editing this book.

PREFACE

I was so touched by the movie *I'll Be Me,* the story of country singer Glen Campbell's Alzheimer's journey. I appreciated the courage his family demonstrated in sharing with America something that is very private. I believe going public touched many people to help them understand themselves and a loved one who has Alzheimer's disease.

This outstanding film portrayed the progression of the disease and what the family and friends did to support Glen.

The one thing that was left out of the film was the impact Alzheimer's had on the lives of his family. This book is what it is like to be a caregiver.

I never applied for the job of caregiver. I wasn't qualified. I had no training, no experience and no concept of what I was in for. Circumstances beyond my control thrusted me into this role and I began my journey. I was focused on taking care of my mother who had dementia. I started out as a long distance caregiver.

It wasn't until years later when my wife was diagnosed with dementia that I experienced how tempestuous my journey would become. It was like going to war with no battle plan for offense or defense and having no training, equipment, support and no hope for a sustainable victory. Through it all I have found joy, peace, grace, love, and fulfillment in the role of being a caregiver.

I wrote this story about my thirty-five years as a caregiver to encourage veteran and new caregivers alike. Veteran caregivers will understand these experiences and will giggle at the humorous side of dementia and perhaps a little moistening of the eyes with memories of their own heartaches. I hope that new caregivers may find information and encouragement that will open their minds to what may lie ahead in their own relationships to avoid the pitfalls that I fell into and capitalize on the positive themes and messages that were given to me and I pass on to you.

CHAPTER 1

We Didn't Know

It was three o'clock in the morning. I was sound asleep when something shook me. I awakened and when I opened my eyes all I could see was a bright white light. A deep voice from above asked, "What is your name?" I answered, "Glen."

Adrenaline surged throughout my body, but my mind was a blur. I don't know what God's voice sounded like, but I didn't think it was Him and He knows my name anyway. Then my eyes focused on a shiny badge and the stern look on a police officer's face. He asked me to get out of bed and I put on my robe.

He walked me into the living room and I saw another officer standing by my wife who was fully dressed. With eyes wide opened and nostrils flaring, she shook her finger at me and screamed, "Arrest that man or take me to jail and put me into protective custody. He is not my husband!"

I was stunned. This was no time to argue. I just stood there speechless. The hurt began to seep in as my brain reacted. I've been married to this woman for fifteen years and now she denies knowing me. How can this be? I'd heard of this happening to others, but why me?

The officer spoke softly to Carol and applying his *Verbal Judo* training, deescalated her high level of fear and anxiety. After she settled down, he assured her that she was safe.

The officer told me she had called 911 and reported a strange man was in her bed. I showed him my identification and explained that she had dementia. The officer told her that he believed I was her husband and asked if it would be okay to let me sleep in the guest bedroom. She reluctantly agreed. The officers left and we retired to separate bedrooms.

I didn't sleep much the rest of the night. My mind raced. How could I continue to be her caregiver when she didn't know me and was hysterically afraid of me? This wasn't the first time she didn't know me, but now she was calling the police. What should I do? What is happening to my wife and what about me? What is my future going to look like? How did I ever end up in this situation?

I laid in bed and began to relax, but couldn't fall asleep. My mind drifted back to earlier years, to open my mind and reconnect with who I am and where I came from and how did I come to this point in my life. This was no dream.

Mom and dad were born in 1908 and grew up on the prairie south of Wichita, Kansas when automobiles began to replace the horse and buggy. They were members of the Greatest Generation (a term coined by Tom Brokaw.) They were the children of sharecroppers during World War I and were educated in a one room school house. They married in 1929, the year when American financial institutions collapsed and the Great Depression began. The impacts of that tumultuous time affected them in many ways that we don't understand today. The culture of their early days as well as their family histories molded their perspectives, just as our culture and upbringing has molded us.

Mom and dad moved to Denver, Colorado with my sister Arlene in 1937. I was born in 1941 just before America entered World War II. Our family was typically American with a hard working father who provided for us and a mother who nurtured Arlene and me. We never heard the words: "I love you or I am proud of you." Affection was never verbalized, but demonstrated by being protected, provided for, and being disciplined. My parents were my first caregivers. I learned obedience was a better alternative to spankings.

Dad was my role model who taught me how to fish, hunt, and be a provider for my family. Mother was a stay at home mom until I was in the fifth grade and then she went to work outside the home. Dad was a mail carrier for the Post Office for nearly thirty years.

Arlene and I never had an intimate relationship with our parents. We were raised in a Christian home and grew up going to church. Our faith was not in a shallow social gospel, but one in which we had faith in a living God and believe He revealed Himself in the Bible so that we might get to know Him.

We knew we were loved, but we never had any serious talks about life with them. Both mom and dad were strong-willed and had controlling natures. We couldn't wait to graduate from high school and move away from home. In spite of mom and dad's objections, Arlene married right out of high school. I went on to college.

Even after we left home, our folks continued to control us by making demands to follow their guidance. Arlene and her husband moved to California to escape their control.

When I went to college they paid my expenses for the first two years. As long as they paid my expenses, they had control of my life. I had worked many jobs since I was a boy and by my junior year I was financially independent. I met my future wife Beth and when we announced our engagement dad told me he was going to tie up my savings account to insure I graduated. His name was on my savings account because I wasn't an adult until I turned twenty-one.

Dad would only allocate my money toward my school expenses. I was angry because I had earned and saved all that money. I was hurt, because he didn't trust me. Before he could take action, I withdrew all my savings. We married after I graduated, which was our plan to begin with.

I graduated from Colorado State University in 1963 with a Bachelor's Degree in Wildlife Management. I followed my dream to be a Wildlife Officer for the Colorado Division of Wildlife. My first assignment took us 300 miles across Colorado to Cortez in the Four Corners. The distance between mom and dad enhanced our relationship. Our daughter Lois and son Ralph were born in Cortez. In 1966 I was transferred to Creede near the headwaters of the Rio Grande River.

After dad retired from the Post Office, they left the congestion of Denver in 1970 and moved to the quiet town of Meeker in Northwest Colorado. Dad loved fishing the White River and the high lakes in the Flattop Wilderness Area. I asked dad why they were moving to Meeker rather than moving closer to Beth and me. Dad said he wanted to maintain a buffer between mother and us. He was concerned if they lived too close, mother's behavior would be a source of friction that no marriage needed. It was a 300 mile drive on winding mountain roads from Creede to Meeker.

I thought their move was a good one, but I detected more than the usual amount of tension between mom and dad. During one of our visits in 1975 dad confided in me, "I can't stand to live with her or to live without her." Divorce for their generation had a stigma and was not an alternative for them. Their marriage had become one of accommodation rather than love. Some tension had always been in their marriage, but mom's behavior was changing.

Dad was concerned that she was becoming sloppy in the way she dressed, which was so unlike her. It could be normal aging, but she was becoming more forgetful and paranoid. We didn't recognize this as dementia and at that time nobody ever heard the word. People used the word "senility" to describe what we consider symptoms of dementia now. This as well as other mental disorders had a social stigma people just didn't talk about. People with mental illnesses were incarcerated in the state mental hospital in Pueblo, because nursing homes were few and far between and ill equipped to handle them.

When mother was about seventy years old we detected that she was becoming paranoid and beginning to hallucinate. She told us a little neighbor girl had broken into their garage and stole

some things.   Dad just shook his head "No."
Another time she claimed she saw a man sitting in
their garage and smoking marijuana. We knew she
had no idea of what the drug smelled like, let alone
seeing a stranger sitting in the garage.

In addition to forty-nine years of disharmony,
dad was coping with mother being in the early
stages of dementia.   We had little idea of the
circumstances he was enduring. Her behavior was
becoming less rational and their relationship was
becoming more strained.

Dad was diagnosed with leukemia in 1974 and
mother became his fulltime caregiver.   He was
suddenly dependent on her, which added to his
anxiety. Mother was under increased responsibility
for his care and hated to see him suffer. She drove
him to his doctor appointments in Grand Junction
a hundred miles away. She was a good caregiver.

During this time I became very close to dad.
The past was behind us and we could talk for hours
about anything at all. He bravely fought the disease
and tried to live a normal life, which included tying
trout flies and fishing. He so loved fishing and he
came home from his last fishing trip with one of
his finest catches. The next day he died from
leukemia in October of 1978.

We soon realized how dad had been a stabilizing
influence to mother.   He took care of her and
before he was diagnosed with leukemia, we never

dreamed he would die first. After he died the boundaries came down. She was alone and could do anything she wanted to do. Her behavior was rather bizarre at times. She lived in her own world.

Mother coped pretty well most of the time. I couldn't differentiate between personality and demented behavior, which really wasn't important anyway. She had trouble with her dentures fitting and went to several dentists. She would ask a total stranger if he or she liked their dentist. Then she would make an appointment and drive as far as to Denver for an appointment. She was able to find her way and paid thousands of dollars trying to get a perfect fit for her dentures, but to no avail.

On one of her ventures to Denver, mother drove into a construction zone and totaled her car. She was unhurt and stayed with a brother-in-law until I could return her to Meeker. Mother was losing her inhibitions.

My uncle called and said that in the early evening they were watching television and mother announced, "It's time to go to bed." She proceeded to take her clothes off and stood there stark naked in front of them.

"I was shocked, he said, but frankly, her strip tease wasn't much of a turn on." I had to laugh. I didn't know it then, but the loss of inhibitions can be a symptom of dementia.

I drove to Denver and took mom back to Meeker. Within a few days she called and told me she bought a new red Chevy Spectrum. She became known as the little lady in the little red car. People soon learned to be on the lookout.

Mother's sight was failing and she was diagnosed with macular degeneration. Although the ophthalmologist explained that eye glasses would not help her vision, she would not accept his diagnosis and process the information. She had her mind made up to find the perfect ophthalmologist and he could restore her vision with the perfect pair of glasses. She could not accept reality and went to every eye doctor she heard of, but to no avail.

Mother had wonderful neighbors and we began to get information from them that mother was beginning to fail in several ways. Mother confided in them and they kept me informed. She called me and said the phone company was threatening to disconnect her phone, because she wasn't paying her bill which amounted to $450 in one month. She denied making so many calls. She gave me the number of the phone company representative. I learned mother made calls all across the nation which were wrong number connections. The representative said she talked to a man in Phoenix, Arizona who said a nice lady had dialed a wrong number and talked to him for more than an hour.

She had indeed made all the calls that she had denied making.

I told mother she would have to pay the bill or have her phone disconnected. The phone was her connection to her friends, relatives, and family. Losing her phone would not be unlike what the loss of our computers, cellphones, and email would mean to us today. I asked her if it would be okay if I had all her bills sent to me and I'd take the burden off her shoulders. A close friend in Meeker had mother's confidence and along with mother's attorney convinced her to give me Power of Attorney to help manage her affairs. She reluctantly agreed and that was one hurdle behind us, but there were so many more to overcome in the years ahead. We were fortunate that mother was still lucid enough to realize she needed help and trusted me to handle some of her affairs.

Having been a survivor of the Great Depression, mother never forgot her survival skills. In some ways she never recovered from handling the hardships of the time. If a doctor sent her a bill and she thought it was too much, she sent him the amount she would have paid him during the Depression, and thought that was enough. Why she didn't have bill collectors knocking at her door was amazing to me.

I've heard it said that an active senior is one who is able to project guilt up to 2,000 miles. Mother was very good at it. One of the neighborhood spies called and asked, "Do you have any idea of what your mother is doing? She is painting her house!" Oh boy!

Mother called, "Guess what I'm doing?" I asked, "What are you doing mother?" She said, "I'm painting my house, because it costs too much to hire it done. Would you come up and help me finish?" You need to understand, I was raised to obey my elders and to honor my mother and father. I wasn't thinking rationally when I answered, "Yes." Mother was barely five foot tall and all I had to do was "finish," which really meant I would paint most of the house. She insisted I use her four-inch paint brush and then I was supervised by a half blind boss who was hard to please. This taught me a lesson about long-distance caregiving. You have no control and have no idea about what is really going on. We were fortunate that mother had neighbors who had witnessed her mental decline and kept a watchful eye on her.

Mother told me she was giving large sums of money away to avoid paying taxes and we were concerned about her giving away too much, because we thought someday she was going to need every penny to pay for long term care. Beth and I asked a psychiatrist how to deal with her giving away so much money and shared with him our concern about her memory failing and not living in reality. The only thing he told us was to help her to maintain her independence for as long as possible. He made a good point, but there is a time when the family is going to have to face the harsh reality of becoming caregivers. He never mentioned the word "dementia." He never explained anything about the progression of her behavior and what we as caregivers would be facing up the trail.

I pause here to pay tribute to the Meeker Police Department and Si Woodruff, the Chief of Police in the 1990s. Si's leadership, his police officers, and staff provided the best of service and protection to the city of Meeker. The relationship of his department to the citizens of the community was a prime example of excellence in law enforcement.

Si called me at home and said, "You've got to do something about your mother's driving." How do you get the car keys when you live 300 miles away? This was by far a greater challenge than having a wild teenage driver in the family. He said he couldn't continue having his officers follow mother around town resetting mailboxes and posts she either backed into or ran over. All the 'granny dents' in her car did give it a certain personal touch. Everybody in town knew who was driving and to avoid the little lady in the little red car. When the neighbor kids played in the street they posted a lookout. When mother came driving down the street, the alarm was sounded and the kids ran for safety.

For her own protection Si wanted to have mother reexamined by the Division of Motor Vehicles (DMV) to take her driver's license away. Her license was about to expire so it was easily arranged. Mother called and said she was going to get her driver's license renewed. I called the nice lady at the DMV office in Meeker and asked her to flunk mother in any way she could. Mother failed the vision test, but she went to an eye doctor and begged him to change the numbers. He felt sorry for her and gave in to her pleading. He gave her a passing vision grade. He put himself in real jeopardy by falsifying her vision numbers. She returned and flunked the driving test for violating several traffic laws. The State of Colorado allowed an individual to take the test five times.

Mother called and said the examiner flunked her and she was going to go to Craig and get tested there. So I called ahead and warned the examiner that a friend was driving mother so she could take the driving test. I told him the Meeker Chief of Police and I wanted her to lose her driver's license as a matter of public safety. Later, I found out she nearly ran over a pedestrian. Two down and three to go.

Mother always called to tell me when she was going to the DMV. She had a friend who reluctantly drove mother's car to the DMV offices. I called ahead to the offices in Glenwood Springs, Rifle, and Grand Junction. Mother lost her driver's license and the citizenry of Meeker and surrounding area were a lot safer as was our mother.

We were elated that she lost her driver's license, but were really insensitive to her feelings of failure, disappointment, and the "What do I do now?" panicky feeling. Mother needed support and understanding and partly due to our being so far away, we were unable to accommodate her need for transportation. She was totally dependent on her friends and neighbors. There was no public transportation in Meeker as is the case in most small towns.

Staying ahead of mother has a glint of humor now, but to thousands of families dealing with mobility issues, this is no laughing matter. In our highly mobile society the driver's license is not only a permit to drive, but it is symbol at the very core of independence and control. We grieve such losses. We were fortunate that mother lived in a small town where everybody looked out for the elderly, but there is a limit to imposing responsibility upon neighbors and friends.

Mother lived alone for fourteen years after dad's death. During that time we began to see more behavioral changes and it was becoming obvious it might not be long before it would be unsafe for her to live alone and far away from us. We were facing the reality that one of these days we were going to have to place her into a care center, but at what point should we do it? Mother's independence was endangering her and others around her.

It still boils down to making the decision sooner or later. Arlene was a Licensed Vocational Nurse (LVN) in California and had worked in nursing homes for several years. She said someday the decision would, "fall into our laps." A lot of things were going to happen before this fell into our laps and we still needed to plan ahead. I didn't know what resources were available. Although mother had not been diagnosed with dementia, she began demonstrating classic symptoms of the disease.

One night mother called and said some people were under her house having a wild party and playing loud music. She called the police, but by the time they arrived the party was over. I explained to her that those folks could only be about two-feet tall in the crawl space. She said it didn't matter if they were that short, they were making too much noise. It didn't dawn on me that we were in two different worlds and she was unable to enter my reality. It took me many years to learn that reasoning with a demented person is a no-win argument. The police reports began to stack up.

Mother called the police one winter night to report someone knocking on her windows and trying to break into the house. A police officer who lived across the alley ran through the snow and found no tracks around her house. It didn't matter if there were no tracks in the snow, they were still knocking on her windows and scaring her. We didn't take her to a neurologist for tests and I'd never heard the phrase, "mild cognitive impairment." Her ability to take in new information and process it to make wise decisions was fading.

Mother had a beautiful yard and hated dandelions. One day she was spraying weeds. Some of the spray drifted onto her beloved garden. A couple days later the garden plants were about dead. She called the city police, the sheriff, the county agent, and the EPA. The county agent told her the herbicide 2-4D had killed the garden. Mother told the policeman she had seen the next door neighbor enter her yard after dark and spray her garden. No amount of reasoning could change her mind, but lacking proof, nothing was done. The neighbor eventually moved.

Mother decided her sidewalk from the street to the house needed to be replaced. She hired a man for the job. He removed the old concrete, made new forms, and poured a new sidewalk. Mother looked at it and with her poor eyesight said it wasn't level and she refused to pay. When I found out, I called the good man and asked him the amount of the bill and he said to forget it. I felt guilty for the way she treated people.

There are some real advantages to living in a small town. The people of Meeker took care of our mother. She looked out for the people of Meeker as well. The city council was considering putting fluoride into the town water supply. Mother had heard there were potential negative effects of fluoridation. She put together a petition and started through the neighborhood gathering signatures to stop fluoridation. Who could turn down this little lady? She presented her petition to the city council, which delayed the decision.

Taking mother to eat at a restaurant was always an adventure. Sometimes it was funny like the time we were standing in line to be seated and this very tall biker man with all his tattoos, shaggy hair, long beard, leather jacket, and a mean look, stood next to us. I avoided eye contact and felt rather intimidated. Mother looked up at him and never being at a loss for words asked, "How's the weather up there?" He smiled down at her and in a deep raspy voice said, "Oh, about the same as down there ma'am." The people around us chuckled. Nobody else had the nerve to say anything to him.

Another time mother finished a nice meal and proceeded to remove her false teeth and swish them around in her glass of water. The waitress stood there aghast. I just looked the other way. We never knew what she was going to do and it wasn't always funny.

Mother made an ugly scene in another restaurant. Beth and I escorted her to the parking lot while Arlene went back into the restaurant. The manager was chewing out our waitress. Arlene told the manager the waitress did a good job and our family owed her an apology for mother's behavior.

We were so embarrassed by mother's demented behavior at times, but never gave it a thought about her feelings. We didn't express compassion and love. All she could sense was our disapproval and rejection. We tried to shame her into having acceptable behavior, just like she had done to us when we were children.

We tend to shun people who have dementia or any kind of disability, because we don't know how to communicate. People and especially those with dementia, often live lonely lives. After mother lost her driver's license she walked alone downhill to the senior citizen lunches at the Fairfield Senior Citizen Center. People were afraid to sit next to her for fear she would make up stories about them. After lunch she started walking up hill to her house and someone would usually stop and give her a ride home. Even though friends and neighbors dropped in on her, she lived a lonely life the last few years that she was in Meeker. Living alone can contribute to the onset of dementia, by living in the past, bringing it into the present, and hallucinating.

Mother enjoyed having visitors, as long as they obeyed her rules. One of our cousins and his wife brought their two boys, who were in diapers, for a visit. She asked to wash some diapers, but when it came to using the electric dryer mother said, "No, you hang them outside on the clothes line (even though it was freezing outside.) "It costs money to run the dryer."

Mother never had an automatic clothes washer and dryer until they moved to Meeker. Up until then she washed clothes in an old Maytag ringer washing machine. She made her own laundry soap from a concoction of Boraxo, lye and mixing them with the rendered fat from elk and deer that dad killed. She filled a thirty gallon barrel with homemade soap. When that supply ran out it was quite an adjustment for her to buy laundry detergent, because it costs money.

Mother had something against people taking showers. When anyone visited over night she hung an "out of order" sign on the shower head and told everyone they had to take baths in the tub. I still don't know if these behaviors were from her personality or becoming symptoms of dementia. I couldn't put my finger on a single event or series of events and say the line has been crossed into dementia.

You may have noted I often use the phrase, "symptoms of dementia." There are many causes of dementia and the disease can manifest itself in a wide range of symptoms. AD is one of the major causes of dementia that presents itself as memory loss and physical deterioration being the most common symptoms. The final diagnosis of Alzheimer's is done at autopsy.

One of the 'last straws' came when my wife and I went to spend a couple days with mother. When we went into the house, mother immediately lit into Beth for stealing her knitting needles. I stepped into the fray as Beth stood there taking the verbal abuse.

I screamed, "How dare you accuse my wife of stealing!" I don't know the difference between a conniption and a hissifit, but I know I had either one or the other. I 'flew off the handle,' picked up our suitcases and we stomped out the door. I was mad and Beth was hurt. I had no empathy for mother and my words and body language hurt her deeply. It is difficult to have empathy for a person who is attacking you, but I would learn.

Had I not stood up for my wife, mother would have driven a wedge between us. In dealing with dementia, there is a time when you have to be firm and tell a loved one they are out of line. The chances are however, that a reprimand will be forgotten about as soon as it's spoken. The hurt may last for days. Knitting needles were not important, but attacking one's integrity is an issue or at least I thought it was. We just didn't understand some common symptoms of dementia such as paranoia, misplacing items, and accusing people of stealing.

When we got home, my mother-in-law, who lived close to us, said mother had called her and wanted to know if Beth had given her the knitting needles. She told mother neither of them knitted. Mother told her Beth stole the needles to sell them, because they were worth a lot of money. A few weeks later mother called and no mention was ever made about the knitting needles. The issue died.

I look back now and understand why I reacted the way I did. I couldn't accept her reality no more than she could accept mine. I had no respect for her feelings that indeed weren't based on reality, but I couldn't change them. I reacted out of my sense of love and protection for my wife and reacting the way I did was justified anger in my mind. Demented people often attack and abuse the one they love the most and are most dependent upon, because they are the closest. I would learn there are better ways to react and handle such volatile situations.

CHAPTER 2

The Time Had Come

I got a promotion and we moved from Creede to Montrose, Colorado in 1988, which brought us to within 175 miles of Meeker. Mother was out of control. She was going to different doctors and stockpiling prescriptions. The doctors didn't know what other physicians were prescribing. At the time we didn't have a clue that she was doing this.

Mother was becoming more dependent on her neighbors and friends. She had lost her driver's license and was going blind. She was beginning to accept the reality that she needed help. On her own she decided to have someone come live with her on a trial basis. A young lady moved in with mother to help her with housekeeping chores and offer some companionship in trade for room and board. She was a local young lady of excellent reputation. The attempt to infuse some stability into mother's life lasted less than a week. Mom's paranoia kicked in and she accused her caregiver of stealing. She had to leave to protect her own reputation.

It was becoming very apparent that mother wouldn't be able to live alone much longer. We knew living in Arlene's home in California or our home in Montrose would not be acceptable to our spouses. It was not realistic to move mother to California either. We really didn't discuss alternatives and Beth and I had no problem becoming her caregivers, as long as she was in a care facility.

I visited a couple assisted living facilities. When I described mother's symptoms I was advised that they could not provide the level of care she needed. I visited several local nursing homes in and near Montrose. It is one thing to visit someone in a nursing home, but I found it a completely different experience when I took a tour with the anticipation of placing mother into such a facility. The sounds of residents calling for help, screaming, crying, and other expressions of desperation filled my ears. The empty stares in their faces, people sound asleep and slumped in wheel chairs, and residents moving along slowly behind their walkers took a toll on my emotions. I told myself mother wasn't all that bad off to be placed there. I knew I was lying to myself which is also called "denial". The guilt began to take over my own cognitive ability to think rationally. If I really love my mother, how could I do this to her?

Spouses, adult children, relatives, and friends may have differing opinions which are filtered by distance, frequency of being around a loved one, and their long term relationships. Worse yet is the caregiver who had promised to never place the loved one into a nursing home and now he or she is faced with the reality that there may be no other safe alternative. A loved one's mental condition will deteriorate to the point at which a caregiver can no longer provide the level of care required to sustain them. Placing someone into a facility is not based on emotions, but rather out of desperation because you love them. Caregivers put up with a lot of inconvenience and messy situations, but when your own physical and emotional strength begin to deteriorate, you lose the ability to care for a loved one. This happened to me years later.

I was most fortunate to have a sister who was not only a LVN, but one who worked in nursing homes. She had an understanding of caregiving from the medical and institutional aspects of care. She was also a caregiver for her mother-in-law whose last days were in their home as well as caring for their oldest son. She understood what I was going through and I had her support to make decisions. I consulted her and trusted her judgement on the issues of mother's care.

Sadly, some caregivers don't have unity among siblings, relatives, and friends. This can be a good time for a family to seek counseling, to resolve conflict before it comes time to make the decision regarding long term care. I am insinuating that everyone will sooner or later end up in a care facility. This is simply not the case. Most elderly people are taken care of at home until they die, given the support from family and community.

It was becoming more and more dangerous for mother to live alone. I had been checking into several nursing homes and found most of them had waiting lists, and only one had an Alzheimer's secure unit (locked inner door). I was attending a conference in Denver when a secretary entered the room and called my name. I about panicked. She handed me a note with an emergency message to call home.

Mother had fallen and suffered a painful compression fracture of a vertebra. Somehow she crawled to her desk, pulled the phone to the floor, and called 911. When the EMTs and police arrived they found her on the floor, but they also discovered she nearly started a fire in the kitchen. She came close to burning her house down.

I called Arlene and she arranged a flight from California. I left the conference and headed home. In addition to a compressed spinal fracture, the doctor in Meeker diagnosed mother with "Senile Dementia with Symptoms of Alzheimer's Disease." The doctor told us she could only hold mother for a couple more days, and mother needed to be in a rehabilitation unit of a nursing home. I was glad that I had already contacted Valley Manor Care Center in Montrose, because they had the only Alzheimer's care unit in a six county area and I had already given them a 'heads up'.

The Meeker doctor arranged mother's transfer to Valley Manor. This was the moment of truth for Arlene's prediction: "This [decision] will fall into our laps." The Valley Manor staff prepared for mother's transfer. The three of us talked to the doctor at the Pioneers Medical Center in Meeker. She very wisely told us to take mother directly to the nursing home and under no circumstance allow her to return home. She explained if we had allowed mother to go home, we would have had great difficulty, even court proceedings, to place her into a nursing home. Mother never saw her house again.

The doctor told mother she needed to be in a rehabilitation facility for her back to heal. I found it important for mother to know that a doctor was responsible for placing her into a nursing home. The doctor and everybody else were the bad guys and I was just her loving son who wanted to see to it that she was taken care of. Her pain was severe enough that she didn't argue. We made her as comfortable as possible for the trip to Montrose. The transition into the nursing home went smoothly for a couple months.

While mother was settling into her new environment, the three of us returned to mother's house and began the cleaning process in order to put it on the market. Mother's closest friend met us and told us to search the house for money. Mother most likely used her Depression era survival skills to hide money in case the banks failed again. We spread out. I searched the bedroom which was her 'inner sanctum.' During my search I lifted her mattress and there was a plastic bag full of $20 bills neatly bundled with rubber bands. I called Arlene and Beth to help me count $15,000 in cash. Needless to say, we intensified our search, but didn't find any more money.

I went down to mother's bank. I showed the banker my Power of Attorney and he was glad to see me and yet not so glad. The bank had been using her money without paying interest. He explained that he tried to talk mother out of it, but she insisted in putting $60,000 into a non-interest bearing checking account to avoid paying so much income tax to the IRS. She did this over the previous fourteen years when Certificates of Deposits (CDs) were paying from 10 to 12% interest. I closed her other accounts and went to a financial planner to invest and open an account in a local bank in Montrose.

When we cleaned mother's medicine cabinet Arlene was shocked. Being a medical nurse she knew what she was looking at. Mother had a stash of medicine. She had even kept dad's leukemia and arthritis drugs as well as all his other medicines. Some were more than twenty years old. When we cleaned her cupboards we found old cans of food bulging and were undoubtedly spoiled and mold was growing in the refrigerator.

I contacted a realtor and put mother's house up for sale. In a short time we got an offer from a man who was looking for a house for his mother. He asked if the furniture, appliances, and anything left in the house could be included in the purchase price. This arrangement saved us from having an auction or estate sale. It worked out for both our families. God is the Master of Detail and He certainly had a hand in settling mother's affairs. Some would call this coincidence, I don't.

We said farewell to mother's neighbors and thanked them for their understanding and patience. They shared some humorous stories about mother which had us laughing with them. We could never fully express our gratitude.

When mother's pain began to subside, she thought she would be going home. This was the beginning of those three words I've heard repeated thousands of times by residents in care centers, "TAKE ME HOME!" Sometimes it was an order and other times it was a plea to take her home, because, "I have business affairs to take care of." During one of her lucid moments we sat down and I explained that doctors said she should no longer live alone and needed the level of care provided by Valley Manor. I told her we were already looking after her best interests. I told her I found the money under the mattress. She looked relieved. I asked her if she had hidden any other money in the house and she said she hadn't. I told her that I sold her house and I had gathered all her financial assets and invested them so the interest would pay for her room and board and give her the care she needed. She was able to process that information and accepted what I had to do for her well-being. Living closer to us contributed to her sense of security. I began growing closer to my mother.

CHAPTER 3

The Caring Time

We no more than got mother settled in and I faced a mountain of paperwork. Mother was receiving Social Security and a survivor benefits from dad's years of working for the Post Office. I had to prove I had Power of Attorney to handle her affairs. They made request after request to document the need to place mother into a nursing home and why I should handle her affairs. They weren't satisfied with my Durable Power of Attorney status. The state had not yet required Medical Power of Attorney.

Si Woodruff sent me copies of an inch thick file of police reports documenting mother's paranoia and a letter describing the dangerous circumstances of her living alone. Si also recommended she be placed in a skilled nursing facility. Her doctor wrote a letter stating that mother had dementia and should be placed into a nursing home. My input seemed rather inconsequential.

After everything was approved, I submitted monthly reports to government offices documenting that I was administering mother's investments and benefits to pay for her care. When we first placed mother, her Social Security and dad's survivor benefit along with the interest from her assets paid for her care, but as the cost increased every few months, we gradually used the principle.

The nursing home had its share of 'hoops' to jump through. Doctors provided her medical records so the nursing home staff had that history. I filled out an extensive questionnaire which provided a family history as well as information about her employment, her likes and dislikes, children, marriage, fears, joys, and many more areas. The questionnaire helped the staff understand that she was more than an emptying shell of a person, but she was quite a lady with many life experiences to be admired. I had many conferences over the years to listen to staff evaluations as well as opportunities to share my perspective and concerns. Although I was sometimes asked how I was doing, there was no caregiver support. The home caregiver and family are still involved, but in a different role and there was no provision for our needs, other than sponsoring a support group.

Mother adjusted quite well to her new environment. Having lived alone for fourteen years, she thrived in her new social environment. She enjoyed many of the activities and she especially loved music. Beth played the piano whenever she went in to see mother. When a pianist came to entertain, mother loved to dress up in her costume with top hat, tails, and her big glasses with a big plastic nose. She gave sheet music to the pianist and sang *"Thanks for the Buggy Ride"*- all three verses from memory, on key, and tempo. Her favorite song was *"In the Garden"*. She brought some joy and smiles to other residents and the staff.

Music is a powerful therapy. One of the most amazing demonstrations of music therapy happened one day when I was visiting mother. A lady started playing the piano. A gentleman rose out of his chair like a robot and walked across the floor to a lady and offered his arm. She took ahold of him, got to her feet, and they began to waltz around the commons area. It was absolutely amazing and beautiful. When the music stopped, she went back to her chair, and he to his and they both bowed their heads and looked like they had gone to sleep.

There were many musicians who donated their time on a regular basis to entertain the residents. Several churches provided services and music. A chaplain visited with residents with attention to their spiritual needs.

In some ways mom was like her own mother when it came to bringing a little joy, some smiles and even a little laughter. We visited my grandma who was about ninety-two years old in a nursing home in Wellington, Kansas in the 1970s. I met with the administrator and asked how my grandma was doing. She replied, "Your grandma is the sparkplug of life in this place." She took us to a commons area where the residents were playing Bingo. There was my grandma helping "the old folks" play Bingo. Grandma walked us to her room and I asked her how she liked it there. She raised her voice and said, "It's kind of bad around here when we have to cheer up the help." The lady who was mopping the floor in the hallway about dropped her mop laughing. How precious it is to come to life's end being a blessing to others.

Mother was helpful to her neighbors. I went in one day and she came out of another room and waved at me to come to her. She told me, "Go over to Safeway and bring in all the boxes you can. I'm helping this lady pack her things, because she is going home. The nurse stood there desperately shaking her head and mouthing the word, "No." I told mother that Safeway didn't give away boxes anymore. I hated myself for lying, but learned about the "therapeutic lie." This is a dangerous thing to do, because down deep the person may know the truth and not be able to express the fact that he or she knows you are lying. Avoid the therapeutic lie as this can cause distrust, just like it does with those who don't have dementia.

A few of mother's friends came by to visit. One challenged my authority and motivation to place her into the nursing home. When people visited for a short time, she was very skillful in putting on an act and one would logically ask: "Why is she in this place?" Those who spent a little more time soon detected the memory lapses and the 'cogs' in her brain weren't quite meshing. I witnessed members of other families in conflict with nurses over the care of their loved one. Some were in denial about their loved one's condition and even blamed staff for symptoms of dementia, much like some parents blame a child's behavior on a teacher.

For several years I took mother off the unit for rides in the mountains. She enjoyed seeing the aspen leaves change color in the fall, and sometimes she saw elk, deer, and other wildlife. I brought her to our house and she got to hold her youngest great granddaughter and enjoy her grandchildren. She enjoyed the holidays with family. After a few hours though, she would look at her watch and say, "It's time to take me home now."

Mother's eyesight was gradually deteriorating, but she could close her eyes and crochet like a machine. She entered an afghan in the county fair and won a prize. When her macular degeneration worsened, mother began crocheting caps for anyone who came into her room. She brought a lot of smiles to the people around her. After mother died, the staff had a memorial service for her and nearly everyone wore one of her caps. Her eyesight eventually deteriorated to the point that she could only see colors and no images. At this point I didn't take her out anymore.

Mother had surgery after a serious gallbladder attack. She spent several days recovering in the hospital. Unbeknown to me, she was released from the hospital and complained to the discharge nurse that she didn't want to go back to the nursing home. So, the well-meaning nurse, not realizing mother was in a secure unit, said she didn't have to go back and there were plenty of other places she could live. She gave mother a list of care facilities in the area, none of which had a secure unit. When I met mother she had the list in hand and was ordering me to take her to all the other care facilities. It took a couple weeks to get her settled in all over again. She was so proud to display her gall stone that was the size of a pullet egg.

I hated to be the one to complain, but I felt I should bring it to the attention of the administrator, not to discipline the nurse, but to tell her that giving advice can bring complications to a patient and her caregivers.

Women of mother's generation were great cooks and their husbands were used to eating foods seasoned to perfection. Institutional food just doesn't measure up to a new resident's expectations. As we get older our taste buds and olfactory senses change and even familiar dishes don't taste the same. The food tends to be a little bland because some residents are on special diets restricting salt, sugar, and other seasonings. Mother was dissatisfied with the food, but rather than boycotting the meals and refusing to eat, she sent several notes back to the kitchen, "If anyone in the kitchen would like to have some cooking lessons, I would be glad to provide instruction." Evidence of the influence of the Depression surfaced when we discovered mother was hoarding sugar and salt packets. When I went in for a visit she often asked about the price of sugar and other commodities, which were rationed during the war years. I used such questions as 'triggers' for recalling the past and enabling me to open up conversations.

Freedom Hall was the name of the secure unit within the nursing home. Prior to having a secure unit (locked door), wandering patients were often constrained with straps in a Geri Chair. This was a common practice in nursing homes. With the unit secured, patients were free to wander the halls, commons area, and a fenced in backyard. To unlock the door a person had to press four keys in the proper order on a combination keyboard lock.

Mother watched people use the lock and she soon memorized the numbers and sequence and could let herself out. All those years as a bank teller gave her skill in using numbers. Fortunately, she never let any other resident out, but she took her water container and went down the hall to the ice machine, filled it, and returned to the unit and her room.

Mother did as much as she could to take care of herself. Even though the facility did her laundry, she washed her underwear in the sink and hung it on hangers in the window. The display gave her room that

certain personal touch. The staff encouraged her to do what she could for herself. She participated in most activities and when the residents were told that they were going to be able to help plant some flowers in some outdoor planters, mother took charge. She never lost her 'green thumb' ability to grow beautiful flowers. She felt needed and important.

Mother had osteoporosis and one day we think she got out of bed, stood up, her hip broke, and then she fell. Her bone structure was so honeycombed from osteoporosis, the doctors recommended against surgery. So, mother spent the remainder of her life in a wheel chair. She learned to wheel herself around until she became so weak that she needed assistance.

For the last year of her life, mother was in the late stage of dementia. She was unable to feed herself and was so frail. She was moved from Freedom Hall, because she was no longer a flight risk. Sometimes I went in at meal time and helped feed her. I often found her asleep curled up in a fetal position. Yet, when she was awake she knew who I was and had not lost the ability to talk and sometimes tell me what to do. Arlene had been coming once a year from California to visit. Mom always recognized her. I kept Arlene abreast of mother's prognosis so that when she came to visit, she wasn't blindsided by changes in mother's condition.

When we were children, mother mended worn out clothes with patches on our blue jean knees and darned the holes in our socks instead of replacing them. Mother dressed nicely when she was a bank teller. As she slipped into dementia however, she no longer dressed up. She wore loose fitting trousers, which made it easier for the CNAs to help her get dressed. We bought mother new clothes at Christmas and for birthdays. When I cleaned her chest of drawers and closet I found our gifts unopened, because "There is plenty of wear left in this sweater (or whatever)." She couldn't throw anything away, because during the Depression and war years you didn't throw much of anything into the trash.

Arlene comforted me and helped me cope with guilt with the statement: "We have been lovingly responsible." Our family dynamic was important. Arlene knew what it meant to go sleepless night after night and just wearing out day after day. What a blessing it was to be on the same page when it came to making decisions.

During one of Arlene's visits she was able to attend a caregiver support group meeting. A family was complaining about the care their loved one was receiving. Arlene took the floor (learned that from our mother) and asked to speak. She talked to the group from the perspective of a professional caregiver who was nursing their loved one. This family was in a state of denial about their loved one's dementia and could not accept the fact that their loved one was only a shell of the person she had been. Arlene spoke as a family member and used our mother and our relationship as an example of how we dealt with our mother who was no longer the person we had known all our lives. She shared how we supported each other and worked with the staff. Afterwards, the leader of our support group thanked Arlene for mediating a really dicey situation.

It is very important for a primary caregiver who lives with and has sole responsibility for a loved one to have the support of siblings or other family members. In some cases however, distant family members only visit occasionally and either by ignorance or pride are in a state of denial about what it is like living with dementia. It's not only important to keep family members current about a loved one's condition, but also just as important to communicate what a caregiver is going through and the need for respite. A high percentage of caregivers suffer physical and emotional problems and some die before their loved one.

I know of one scenario in which the wife was faced with a sister-in-law who interfered constantly by trying to override the care she was giving to her husband who was in mid-stage dementia. This overbearing sister loved her "little" brother and felt it her role to look after him, totally ignoring his wife. The big problem however, was that she herself was in the early stages of dementia. Her interference was so great that the wife was considering getting a restraining order to keep her from meddling in his care and had to disconnect the telephone. Not all is so rosy on the home front in some cases.

Mother was a masterful manipulator. When she wanted something from me she inferred, "If you love me you will do thus and so." She asked me to sneak medicines such as aspirin or some other medicine into her room. I never smuggled contraband onto the unit. This was one way of proving to herself that she was in control of some part of her life. It got to the point that I'd call a nurse or Certified Nurse Assistant (CNA) and ask if it was safe for me to come visit, because mother made demands I couldn't deliver on and left her angry and handling her more difficult for the CNAs. She made a list of chores for me to do, just like she did whenever I visited her at home. Just about every visit ended with the demand "Take me home."

One of the coping mechanisms I valued the most was our caregivers support group. The first time I attended a meeting I felt like a lone traveler on the trail. It was like hiking into a camp of sojourners. I was welcomed and laid my 'pack' down for a while. They gave me a cup of water for a thirsty soul and I listened to folks who had been on the trail for a long time. They shared their experiences and encouraged me. I learned how they coped and what they carried in their pack and how to use those tools to cope with dementia.

I joined the group and benefitted so much by being with others who were walking down the same tempestuous trail. We were all at different stages of caregiving and the veterans lifted the spirits of newcomers. I wasn't alone and we learned from each other as well as from professionals in the fields of dementia, financial planning, legal matters, medicine, and research.

It was the personal contact however, when we shared our heart aches, cried tears, and laughed together that meant the most. One man told me he met my mother and had an interesting talk with her. He repeated what mother said about me, "One of these days I gotta kill that boy." Then, another time she told someone, "I never had to spank that boy." I laughed and replied, "You weren't talking to MY mother."

Life was never dull in a nursing home. In thirty-two years of law enforcement I was never seriously assaulted, but one day as I was leaving the unit, a new resident wanted me to let him follow me out the locked door. When I said. "No," and turned my back to him, he hit me over the head with his paperback book. Surprised yes, hurt no. I turned around and asked him to go back to his room with me and tell me some more of his B-17 stories. He piloted B-17 bombers over Germany and enjoyed telling his stories. "B-17" was a memory trigger for him. I wish I would have tape recorded his stories. Even though his short term memory was about gone, he could still remember his glory days.

Within each and every one of us, whether we have dementia or some other disease, there is a respectable and valuable soul which is exciting to discover. It's just a little harder to communicate with someone with dementia, but they still have feelings and the desire to communicate.

Being a caregiver is a very draining experience both physically and emotionally. Well-meaning people encourage caregivers to "Take care of yourself." Just how do you do care for yourself when you are alone with a loved one hour after hour and day after day? It is more complex than a well-intended simple cliché.

I grieved the loss of the same things my mother lost such as independence, spontaneity, mobility, and other freedoms. I was tied down, less likely to do something on the spur of the moment, and not free to go where and when ever I felt like it. Much of this was self-imposed out of guilt. I was also working fulltime.

The danger of storing resentment for the loss of these can build to such a point that the slightest comment can trigger a fit of anger and hurtful words and then comes the guilt and sadness of overreacting. A caregiver needs periodic respite to get away and do something he or she enjoys. A well rounded life is a balance of physical, mental, emotional, spiritual, and social elements. A caregiver can have "flat spots" in any combination of these factors. Like a tire that is out of round, the ride gets pretty bumpy and it wears out the suspension system and weakens other systems until they break. This is just another reason why it is so important to seek professional counseling. The worst scenario is to be so flat one can barely function because of incapacitating depression – aka caregiver burnout.

My life seemed to be going flat in several ways. The State Personnel Board 'bumped' me out of the job which I had been promoted to and my employment was uncertain, our marriage was on the rocks, and I suffered a brain seizure all within a few months. My employment situation improved and I survived the seizure without any further episodes. Our marriage however, ended in divorce. I still had my mother to look after.

CHAPTER 4

Here I Go Again

After our divorce I was still mother's caregiver for the last four years of her life. I went to a divorce recovery class and began to get some balance back into my life. At the conclusion of the class the group decided to start a singles group. My social life became more rounded. After meeting for a year, a new lady joined our group who became our new leader. Carol was a vivacious woman who organized activities and meetings for our group. We began to get acquainted and I felt comfortable around her. Carol had also been divorced.

We started dating. We came from two entirely different backgrounds, but had so much in common. I still had some stress of having been divorced, but my employment situation had improved. One day Carol showed me some pills she took for depression. I didn't know anything about depression.

We married under a tall Ponderosa pine tree in the San Juans Mountains in 1995. When we said our vows we promised to love and be faithful "in sickness and health." The first few months that we were married we continued to get acquainted. I began to learn what it was like to live with my wife who suffered from anxiety and depression and the impact it would have on me.

Carol was born in 1939. She was an only child. Her parents divorced when she was five years old. After the divorce, Carol was not allowed to see her biological father. Her mother was abusive. She disciplined by shunning and wouldn't speak to Carol for several days, causing her feelings of rejection and abandonment which have resurfaced in some symptoms of dementia. Carol was desperate to please her mother. She was given many responsibilities beyond what a little girl would normally have in those days. If a chore such as waxing the floor wasn't polished to perfection, she would have to do it all over again as punishment. She was unable to please her mother, the most important person in her life.

By the time Carol was in college she was suffering from depression. She married, had a son, finished a Master's Degree in Education, and then a daughter was born. A psychiatrist prescribed powerful anti-depression drugs. Depression took over her life to such an extent that her symptoms brought instability to the marriage and to her children. Her husband filed for divorce and was granted custody of their young children. She was granted visitation rights for a few weeks each year, but had no significant time with them. Her husband had moved far enough away with their children that visiting on weekends was out of the question. As a result Carol never had an adult relationship with her daughter who has remained estranged to this day. Her son reconciled with her decades later. Carol was devastated and grieved the loss of her children for many years.

Carol put her life back together and was a masterful teacher before she retired. For many years she had vacationed in the San Juan Mountains of Colorado and when she retired, she moved lock, stock, and barrel to Montrose, Colorado to be close to the mountains. She was an adventurous woman who had rafted through the Grand Canyon and loved to go 'Jeeping' in the San Juans.

We had only been married about six months when I drove up to a stoplight and I experienced double vision. I went to my ophthalmologist and was diagnosed with *Myasthenia gravis*, which in Latin means: "Severe muscle weakness." My eyelids drooped shut and I was becoming unusually weak. My neurologist sent me to the Mayo Clinic in Scottsdale, Arizona for diagnosis and treatment. Carol had to do all the driving and was my caregiver. Fortunately, there is medication for this autoimmune disease, but the side effects for the long term are devastating to the body. I was eventually able to drive and return to work. I've coped with the disease for nineteen years and it has affected my caregiving abilities by zapping my strength.

I retired and we wanted to travel, but I hated the notion of leaving mother just in case she had a sudden downturn and needed me. Even though mother had been in the nursing home for several years, I still thought of myself as being the only one who understood and could be the primary caregiver. Definitions aside, I was no longer the daily caregiver. The nursing home staff encouraged me to take care of myself. The head nurse said as she pointed to the door, "You go and we'll take care of your mother." The first trip we took was not unlike how new parents leave their little one with a baby sitter and just can't relax for worrying about their little one. When we stopped, I often called the nursing home to check on mother. She was in good hands and it took me some time to relax.

As mother neared the end of life, Hospice came to minister those last few weeks. Mother was asleep most of the time, but all of the staff and Hospice caregivers attended to her every need and to mine as well. Mother was a Christian and several times she had expressed no fear of dying. My own faith comforted me as I watched my mother in her last hour. I leaned over to her and whispered in her ear that it was okay to leave and be in the presence of Jesus and I would be okay. I left and within the hour a CNA called and said mother had passed on.

Mother lived for nine years in Valley Manor. I knew mother was slowly dying, but when she passed on I felt a sense of shock. I was prepared and had all of mother's affairs in order. There was a sense of relief that mother was no longer suffering and the same for me as her caregiver. The heavy responsibility was lifted from my shoulders.

My mother died in 2000. During this time I noticed Carol's memory was beginning to fail. We went to a neurologist who ordered an MRI taken of her brain and diagnosed her with 'chronic brain disease.' After further testing, he diagnosed her with 'mild cognitive impairment.' This was devastating news, because the doctor explained that these maladies are often precursors to dementia. Long term depression can also play a role in bringing on dementia. Carol had a double whammy.

Carol began to have chronic fatigue and muscle pain. She could barely get out of bed in the mornings and the pain was incapacitating. I took her to a doctor who said her symptoms were psychosomatic. We went to another doctor and he referred us to an arthritis specialist. He diagnosed Carol with Fibromyalgia, a form of arthritis that affects muscles instead of joints. There was no effective medicine at that time except to control pain.

The Montrose Memorial Hospital offered a class in how to cope with Fibromyalgia. I went with Carol and learned not only how to manage her disease, but also for my own Myasthenia gravis. Carol and I found ourselves not being able to do things we'd always enjoyed doing. Carol loved to sew, but couldn't thread a needle. I enjoyed hiking, but no longer had the stamina. We found ourselves saying, "I should be able to do that." Whether I did this to myself or if someone else reminded me I 'should' be able to do something. My inability to accomplish things I had always done left me with frustration, guilt, and negative feelings.

When I finally accepted my condition, I learned to be more gracious to Carol and to myself. We tried to maintain an active lifestyle and adjust where we could. Carol could no longer do housework and I did most of the cooking. The training we had paid off. Eventually, Carol began having fewer symptoms of Fibromyalgia and it became less of an issue for her care. I learned to slow down and pace myself.

About this same time Carol complained things didn't feel right in her chest. She didn't have any pain or pressure, but I learned she was good at listening to her body. She went to our doctor and he sent her to the hospital to have her fitted with a cardiac monitor. While the nurse was fitting her, BAM! She was rushed into the emergency room. When I got there the ER team and cardiologist were stabilizing her. She had a 95% blockage of the left coronary artery. She was rushed by ambulance to Saint Mary's Hospital in Grand Junction where the cardiac team inserted two stents. The next day she walked out of Saint Mary's.

Two days later we met her son and family in New Mexico and spent a week sharing their vacation. She was amazing. A couple weeks after they went home, we took an extended vacation to British Columbia. We had a wonderful vacation in the northwest and Carol was pain free.

We had just returned a few days before the world changed on September 11, 2001. America lost her innocence that fateful morning when terrorists crashed airplanes into the World Trade Center, Pentagon, and a failed attempt crashed into a Pennsylvania field. In the following weeks the news was flooded with stories related to the attacks. The president deployed U.S. armed forces to Afghanistan.

A short time afterwards Carol woke me up one night and said she had looked down the street and saw an airplane loading up soldiers to go to Afghanistan. She described the plane and even the strobe light flashing on fuselage. I told her she was dreaming and passed it off.

A couple days later we were watching television and she started describing some fungus like substance with tiny flowers growing on her skin, then on the furniture. Her pupils were dilated and she was on the verge of hyperventilating. She told me to start throwing things away which were covered with this substance. Then she saw it growing on me and she was in a full blown, hysterical panic attack. Her description made me remember the 1950s horror movie *"The Thing,"* which featured a mysterious vegetative glob from outer space that was engulfing everything in sight. I tried to comfort her and talk her out of her hallucination, but to no avail. I was up all night with her. She was so consumed with fear and wouldn't let me out of her sight. I was beside myself with worry, fear, and frustration.

The next morning I called her neurologist who arranged for me to take her to a mental health facility for evaluation and treatment. I wasn't allowed to see her for nearly two weeks, but I finally got to talk to her doctor. He verified the brain lesion and also discovered one of her anti-anxiety medicines had become toxic and was causing some of her symptoms. He was backing her down and eventually off that drug.

During those two weeks I was beside myself with fear and anxiety. I felt like I was in a massive trap with no way of escape. I wanted to run away. I even thought of divorce as a way out. I had lost the trail. I saw Tim having coffee at McDonalds. I told him, "I need help!" Tim was a professional counselor who I knew from church. He had a couple free hours in the afternoon.

Tim told me then he didn't fix people, but he walked alongside to guide them through such difficult times. This was the beginning of a twelve-year relationship. The trail of our lives is lined with trail blazers and guide posts whom God places there to protect us, give us guidance, and encouragement to stay on the trail. I don't know how I would have survived without counseling. God knew and sent Tim into my life. I can't emphasize enough that seeking professional counseling for the caregiver is just as important as finding help for a loved one

I was meditating in my Bible in Philippians 3:13 where the apostle Paul wrote, ". . . I have learned to be content in whatever state I am in . . ." I was happy for Paul, but I had a lot more to learn. I wasn't there yet. I talked to God about this and told him I honestly wasn't very content. Then I remembered how Jesus in Matthew 26:39 talked to His Father in the Garden of Gethsemane and in His humanness prayed, ". . .If there is any other way [other than dying for our sins on a cross] let this cup pass from me, nevertheless, not my will, but yours be done. . ." So Jesus is compassionate toward our suffering and pain. Jesus trusted God the Father and is a model for the kind of relationship God wants us to have with him . . . to trust Him.

Then Romans 8:28, 29 came to mind that all things work together for good . . . and verse 29 for the purpose of transforming us into the image of Christ. Well, I know I will never be perfect as long as I'm alive on this earth. I concluded all this suffering I was experiencing is in the end, God's kind of goodness to mature me to be more like Jesus Christ. I believe these verses and trust God is responsible for doing His good in my life through my circumstances. As I reflect back, God has proven Himself to me time and time again and yet so often I think I am in charge and capable of handling my circumstances. Things tend to go sour when I am in charge. I experienced then and ever since, a special kind of grace God provided for my needs and comforting along the way. Trusting God is large part of taking care of myself.

I agreed to bring Carol home from the facility if she would go to counseling with me. She was more than willing. Her condition had improved after getting off the drug which had become toxic. The doctors and staff had been preparing her to come home. She wrote a list of things she would not do such as balancing the checkbook, cooking, and driving, and things that could endanger herself and others. She had another list of things she would do such as clean house, do laundry, read, and garden. We were able to return to some semblance of normalcy. Life smoothed out for several months. We took several more vacation trips and enjoyed life on the road. The counseling sessions addressed the issues we were facing, but the symptoms of dementia such as memory loss, disorientation, and confusion began to increase in frequency and intensity.

It was nice while it lasted, but before long the 'honeymoon' was over as her dementia began to control both our lives. I found myself storing up resentment and 'flying off the handle'. Then I'd feel guilty for my hurtful words and body language, which caused her fear of being abandoned. She had a history of being abandoned and rejected by the most important people in her life.

I found a sheet of paper recently on which she had written about her concern that her memory loss might impact me, and in the back of her mind what it would mean to her. She was afraid I would leave her. She knew she was losing her memory, but was skillful in hiding the fact. She was grieving the loss of such things as memory, mobility, independence, spontaneity, control, and enjoying the things she had always been able to do and it caused her to become angry, frustrated, and sad.

My outbursts were hurting Carol. I was acting out passive/aggressive behaviors. Tim got in my face and told me to, "Cut it out." Through Tim's counsel I learned I was grieving and going through the same stages of grieving the loss of the wife I'd known all these years. I experienced denial, anger, depression, and beginning to accept the reality of what was happening to me. So here we were, two people grieving the same things, but for different reasons.

I wasn't handling the stress of being a caregiver very well at all. I had very poor emotional boundaries. Tim told me to write them down. I listed my boundaries for Carol. Some of them were:

I would do some things that I enjoyed.
I would spend short periods of time away from her
I would spend time with my family
I would not tolerate her manipulating me
I would not tolerate verbal abuse

Boundaries are like fences that tell others the limits of behaviors which will be acceptable and there are consequences to violating my boundaries. I lovingly, but firmly told Carol how to get along with me better. In spite of successfully establishing boundaries, my life was an emotional roller coaster.

Tim recommended to my doctor that he prescribe a mild anti-depressant to help me through all the stress. I wasn't getting enough sleep or eating a healthy diet. I was trusting God, but I couldn't deny my emotions and often cried out to Him to relieve me of my circumstances. Some people want to have a relationship with God, but primarily in an advisory role. I told God I'd like for Him to make my life more comfortable, how to do it, and do it NOW. Instead, because He loves me, He communicated to me, "Trust Me. I see beyond your circumstances."

When it came to the point we would not be taking anymore long trips, I found a part time job driving a shuttle van for a local car dealer. I got out of the house three days a week and I really enjoyed driving and meeting people. Then, one afternoon Carol called my cell phone: "Come get me. I'm in Ruidoso, New Mexico with four boys." Whoa! I knew she was calling from home.

I told my supervisor I needed to go home. When I walked into the living room, she was sitting on the sofa and was very angry. She asked, "Why did you leave me in this flea-bitten motel room with no money and no food?" I asked where the four boys were and she said she didn't know where they had gone. I tried to talk her out of her hallucination and after she inspected the house, not finding the boys, and the familiarity of the house set in, she realized she was at home and settled down. I held her tight. It was a good time to just be silent and be a calming presence. I was so tempted to "fix" her, because men were supposed to solve problems (or so I thought.)

Night after night and day after day the hallucinations were dominating our lives. One night she woke me up and told me to get dressed so we could go to a baby shower. I looked over at the clock and I asked, "They have baby showers at one o'clock in the morning?" She answered, "We had to travel, so get up and get dressed." I asked her who was having a baby and she answered, "**I am!**"

Boy did I wake up! With adrenaline running high, I raised my voice and reasoned with her, "Honey, you had a hysterectomy forty years ago and I a vasectomy at least that long ago. If you are pregnant and we pull this off, we will have Abraham and Sarah's [in the Bible] miracle beat." She responded, "You're right. We'll just have to adopt." I inquired, "Why would we want to adopt?" Her logical and considerate answer, "We can't let the people down who are having the baby shower." Then I asked the big question, "Do you really want to have a baby at our age?" Thankfully, she emphatically answered, "Heavens no!" In relief I said, "Good, me neither. Let's go back to bed." I tucked her in and by the time I walked around and got back into bed she was sound asleep. I didn't sleep too much the rest of the night as the thought of becoming a daddy kept drifting through my mind, sort of like a nightmare.

Another night I awakened as she got out of bed to go to the bathroom. She had begun to wander, so I played opossum and kept track of her. She came back to the bedroom, but didn't get back into bed. I opened one eye and glanced over to see her down on her knees praying. She was praying for me. I teared up. I felt her love. Even in this stage of her dementia, in the depths of her brain she knew God and was talking to Him. Prayer was always comforting to Carol.

Having been a reading teacher for many years, and even though she couldn't remember what she read, she enjoyed reading her Bible. Over the years the scriptures were embedded deep within her and had become a guiding influence in her life. She enjoyed going to church and loved to sing.

Then one Sunday morning we were walking across the parking lot and I reached down to hold her hand and she pulled away and scolded me, "Don't hold my hand. We are not married." This was the first time she said those words. I was shocked, but it was no place or the time to start a discussion on the topic. Needless to say, I wasn't able to concentrate on the sermon. My feelings weren't hurt, but I have to admit that I was in a quandary about how to handle the situation.

When these anecdotes occurred, I brought them up to Tim in counseling sessions and with his education and experience, he'd offer plausible solutions. Otherwise, I'd stay in the same hole spinning my wheels, digging myself deeper into depression. I found it was so important for me to have a confidant whom I could share my heart with. Tim didn't allow the luxury of a pity party, but was always looking deep into my dilemma. I couldn't see the forest because of the trees, but he did.

One evening Carol walked into the living room where I was sitting. She asked, "Did you see the black dog run through the living room just now?" I answered that we didn't have a black dog or any dog. We got into an argument about the existence of a nonexistent dog. Being right or correcting was always counterproductive. It caused me to remember my parents arguing over who was right and it was instilled in me to be "right." I wanted to restore her to my reality.

The most often repeated scenario was, "Did you see mother?" I'd reply, "No, she died twenty-five years ago." Then she came to the verge of tears saying, "She never says goodbye, but just leaves." Carol blamed herself for her mother's treatment of walking out on her. In her dementia she was still trying to please her mother to gain the approval she had so desperately sought all her life.

The majority of her hallucinations were about her mother. She asked me to drive out to our Rural Electric Cooperative (REA) to "pick mother up." (She was a bookkeeper for many years for an REA in Oklahoma.) When Carol was a teenager she chauffeured her mother, because she didn't drive.

Several times Carol told me to go get a quart of milk for her mother, because she always liked a glass of milk before she went to bed. Most of her hallucinations had to do with being responsible toward her mother, which often fell upon my shoulders to act out. I didn't mind going to the store, just to get out of the house. I began to notice Carol didn't hallucinate about people in her past with whom she had good relationships. However, she had been unable to sustain intimate relationships, a common symptom of depression.

One winter night it was bitter cold and she was so worried her daughter was out in the cold. She thought her forty year old daughter who lived in Oklahoma with her family, was twelve years old. She wanted me to call the police to file a missing person's report and we should get in the car and drive around town looking for her. She insisted we not go to bed until her daughter came into the house. I told her we'd better stay in the house and leave the door unlocked and the light on.

I began to understand some of her behavior the more I learned about her past. Her son explained that she took four boys to Boy Scout camp in Ruidoso, New Mexico every year-thus an explanation for the hallucination. The brain was bringing a past event into the here and now.

Carol was an only child growing up in the country on the outskirts of Ada, Oklahoma. At one time her only playmate was a little black dog named "Blackie." She put dresses on Blackie, who was her only playmate. In her hallucination she stood out on the patio and called into the darkness, "Here Blackie, here Blackie. . . " Her heart was breaking and all I was doing at the time was present facts that in no way addressed her pain. She got mad at me when I failed to react the way she thought I should and then I felt either angry or guilty. As her short term memory was fading, those long term feelings from those memories were still there, sometimes in great detail. The dog was real to her and I wasn't about to talk her out of it.

In addition to the constant hallucinating, Carol was becoming more incontinent day and night. I bought a carpet shampooer and laid a plastic rug runner between her side of the bed and the bathroom. Along with diapers, we managed the problem. Our doctor gave her some medication which also helped.

In January of 2005 she woke me up one night and asked, "Who are you?" I answered, "I am Glen, your husband." She accepted my answer. In subsequent days she began to cling to me and I looked for opportunities to get away for even a little while. When I told her I wanted to go to a ball game to see one of my grandkids play, she tried to lay down the law, "It's either me or them." I gave in at first, but then Tim got onto me about my boundaries by encouraging me, "Staying true to your boundaries gives you some stability."

I was wearing out physically, emotionally, and mentally. I kept praying to God to give me strength, but what I think He had in mind was for me to come to the point where I just gave my burden to Him and trust that He was accomplishing His will. He gave me strength to trust Him more. In my case however, the Lord wanted to show me

Sure enough, I was living so low I had to jump up to touch bottom and I was beginning to accept the idea that I needed help. It was hard for me to admit I wasn't the only one who could take care of Carol. I felt like I was about to drown in a sea of horror and a tunnel with no light at the end. Wouldn't you know it, on my next visit to Tim, he perceived my dilemma and directed me to our county social services department to investigate what resources might be available to me. He explained to me that I felt trapped, because I saw no way out, but when I learned what resources were available to me the knowledge sparked a glimmer of hope.

There were a few things between me and the light at the end of the 'tunnel'. I faced an obstacle of paperwork which resembled an unclimbable mountain. It took time, but I worked through the bureaucratic maze with help of local staff in our social services department. I was impressed how they protected the taxpayer's interest and helped me complete all the necessary paperwork. They were patient and understanding. I had to provide such things as a birth certificate, proof of residency, and a myriad of miscellaneous documents. I hired an attorney who updated our wills, Powers of Attorney and reorganized our financial affairs. The light at the end of the tunnel was beginning to glow a little brighter with the completion of each little task.

A case worker came to the house and interviewed us. After the interview she told me we were immediately eligible for some home care assistance (HCA). A health care worker came and inspected the house for safety concerns. Carol was having problems remembering to take her medications when I was at work. HCA furnished us with a mechanical medicine dispenser with an alarm to remind her to take her medications. They also provided a medical alert button she wore around her neck. She could press it for help when I wasn't in the house. She wore the medical alert button for more than a year and then one day she asked me what the button was for. It was obvious that if she fell or needed help, she wouldn't remember to push the medic alert button. Carol had become unable to remember new information.

Because I was working three days a week, HCA sent a home care specialist to be with Carol for a few hours while I was at work. A young lady did some light housekeeping and it was a big help to me and gave me some peace of mind knowing someone was with Carol to keep her safe on those days when I was working. Carol was accepting and trusting of the ladies who came to help.

When I was home Carol became very "clingy" and never wanted me to leave her sight. She resented my going to games to see my grandchildren play ball. It upset her when I stood by my boundaries. She wanted to go with me and be in my back pocket. I was an elder in our church and soon had to ask ladies from the church to sit with her while I attended committee meetings. I had some support, but I had given up my hobbies of hunting, fishing, swimming, photography, travel, and having time alone in order to take care of Carol. I was becoming resentful; not knowing I was grieving the loss just like Carol. The "trail" was becoming obscured at times and I was stumbling.

I was meditating on a verse in the Bible, Philippians 3:13 ". . . *forgetting those things that lie behind I press forward . . .*" This verse challenged me to not let past events define me or limit what I am doing or what I can do. But, what about a person with dementia? I've observed some hallucinations were about people and broken relationships from the past that the brain brings into the here and now. Down deep they want to reconcile a relationship before they die. It is their reality and all the information and reasoning you can present means nothing to them. It was hard for Carol to move forward. I had to make a conscious effort to live day to day, but with hope for the future. She had little to look forward to.

Other hallucinations can be triggered by current events. Even television news and some programing can trigger wild and fearful hallucinations. It is difficult for some to differentiate between reality and fantasy. Carol sometimes thought her dreams were real. This was a dilemma for me until I came to understand that we lived in two different worlds and I was not going to change the fact. I was the only one who could move between our worlds.

Three of the most feared words a husband ever hears from his wife are "We gotta talk." Jeff Foxworthy advises redneck husbands, "Run, you ain't gonna win this one." Likewise, Carol would tell me my three words: "Please unconfused me." I wanted to run because I was doomed for failure. I always tried in the simplest terms to explain the issue so she would understand. It never worked, but I wouldn't give up and tried explaining the issue a different way. Well, the second, third and fourth explanations have to be more complicated and she mixed them altogether. I could explain until the cows come home and get nowhere. It was like both of us were in a clothes dryer and with each explanation it kept turning faster and faster and getting hotter and hotter. She could not process the information and if she did, she forgot it within a minute. It doesn't matter whether she was confused or hallucinating, my reaction was the same. Oh, how I wanted to help her understand. My frustration was as great as hers, because I couldn't get her to understand.

I had a surgery at the Colorado University Hospital in Denver in 2012. It is a huge complex covering several city blocks. A few months later I had a dream that gave me some insight into the fear and confusion dementia must cause.

A Caregiver's Nightmare

I dreamed I had just parked in a parking lot and off in the distance was the huge hospital complex that I needed to go to. I started walking and soon found myself in the midst of a crowd of people. My legs were giving out. I was being bumped around, stared at by some, and mostly ignored.

I must have appeared confused and lost, because a woman came up to me and asked me if I was okay and I told her I needed to get to the hospital, but I was lost. I couldn't see the parking lot to go back to my car and I lost track of the hospital complex. She said to follow her and she would show me the way. I was so relieved, but walking through the crowd she got ahead of me, I couldn't keep up, and I lost track of her. I came out of the crowd and the nice lady had disappeared.

I walked along a path and saw a woman and man sitting on a blanket in a grassy area of a park. I walked up to them and she asked me if I was okay and I told her I was lost and wanted to find the hospital. She asked me, "What does it feel like to be lost? Before I could answer she asked, "How long have you been lost?" "Why do you want to go to the hospital?" A little bit of reality crept into my dream and I thought, "She is practicing Validation Techniques right out of Naomi Feil's Validation book." She wasn't really helping me find the hospital. Finally, she pointed to the direction of the hospital and I walked off and before long I saw the hospital building that I was looking for.

I ran as fast as I could and found the front door locked. Nobody would let me in and then I ran around the whole complex and every door was locked and nobody was around the outside of the building. I beat on the doors. I was alone and in desperation I screamed and woke myself up.

I was out of breath and in a cold sweat. I woke Muffin our little Maltese lying next to me. I rolled onto my side and Muffin licked my face, bringing me back to reality. My pulse slowed and I caught my breath. For the first time I felt down deep in my gut what confusion might feel like to Carol and anyone with dementia. It was beyond scary. I wanted to cry for her. My dream taught me the practical side of empathy toward someone with dementia. When I went to see Carol in the afternoon I swept her up in my arms and kissed her and told her how much I loved her. She said, "I love you too. We ought to get married, but then I know you would have a problem with bigamy."

CHAPTER 5

PACE

I had a lot to learn, but I would soon be exposed to the trailblazers who would teach me how to negotiate the rugged trail ahead. Carol's psychiatrist prescribed several of the drugs that had recently been approved to delay the progression of Alzheimer's disease (AD). None of them worked for Carol, possibly because they were not started early enough. These drugs have helped some people postpone the inevitable progression of the disease if they are started in the early stages of AD. In Carol's case the disease progressed. I had to consider the question: Should I prolong the inevitable outcome? Is it loving to prolong the agony for a loved one? Would I do this for selfish reasons? Am I hanging on when I really need to be letting go? Using memory enhancing drugs is an issue that a family should consult with a doctor and learn the ramifications of such drugs. My decision led us on a different trail.

I don't believe in coincidence or accidents. One day in 2008 our county case worker called to inform me about a new program in Montrose called PACE. I asked her what the acronym stood for and she didn't know. It was brand new, but she had heard it was good and Carol might be eligible for the program. I set up an appointment with PACE. A therapist and registered nurse came to the house to visit. They explained **P A C E** stood for **P**rogram of **A**ll inclusive **C**are of the **E**lderly. The mission of PACE was to provide the highest level of care that could be given at home by enabling home caregivers.

PACE didn't come to Montrose because of some governmental edict. John Fitzmaurice had among other titles in his career, the Regional Development Manager for the Volunteers of America (VOA). VOA owned Valley Manor Care Center a full service facility in Montrose, Colorado providing rehabilitation, memory support, and skilled nursing care. It also owned the Horizons nursing home in Eckert in Delta County about thirty miles from Montrose. VOA is a Christian faith-based service organization whose mission is to reach out and lift up people in need, not just those who have need of a care center.

PACE started in San Francisco in the 1970s. All the PACE centers in the U.S. were in big cities and had never been tried in a rural area. Medicare provided twelve grants of $750,000 for startup pilot programs in rural areas in about 2005. VOA in addition to skilled nursing facilities, had already successfully invested in assisted living facilities and in the home care industry.

John had a vision and convinced VOA to investigate the creation of a PACE center in a rural area, which required looking for new ways to build its business opportunities to serve in the hinterlands. There needed to be something in addition to assisted living and skilled nursing outreach. PACE was a program to facilitate the care of people at home, forestalling the need for being placed in a skilled nursing facility.

To bring PACE to Montrose however, several things had to be in place: a building, a network of health care providers that could be tapped into, and a full service care center. The most difficult hurdle was getting the legislature to approve funding in order to qualify as a Medicaid provider.

The Colorado legislature approved paying PACE 95% of the costs of providing care to qualifying senior citizens from Medicaid. The balance was to come from Medicare and private paying participants. The legislature required a guaranteed 5% savings to Colorado taxpayers and VOA assumed all the risks of financial failure. VOA invested millions of dollars to bring PACE to Montrose. The program had to provide a high quality of care.

VOA had already bought twenty-five acres of land a half a mile from Valley Manor and built the Homestead Assisted Living facility. When the PACE program was brought to Montrose, the

PACE Senior Citizen Care (SCC) center was attached to the building. It was a natural fit. Some physicians however, were skeptical that the level of care would be substandard. Their fear dissipated as doctors and other health care providers participated and witnessed the results of good patient care.

The first few years PACE was on the brink of failure, but by 2015 about 250 participants were enrolled in Montrose and Delta counties. These 250 people would probably be in assisted living or nursing home facilities at greater expense to the taxpayers. Some of the participants do live in VOA nursing homes and PACE continues to manage their care.

Since 2008 VOA expanded the PACE program to its Horizon nursing home in Eckert in Delta County. More recently the small town of Paonia has a satellite PACE program. VOA remodeled the community senior citizen center where PACE programs are available. When a participant needs to see a doctor or have other needs, PACE provides transportation to Horizons or to a contracted health care provider.

As of 2015 there are 114 PACE centers in thirty-two states. There are only fourteen rural centers. Nationally, PACE is saving taxpayers billions of dollars a year and providing participants with a quality of life generally unattainable even in the best of facilities. Thinking outside the box has paid off for caregivers and their loved ones in Montrose and Delta counties.

Since the mission of PACE is to postpone or eliminate the need for going to a nursing home, the major emphasis is to provide home caregivers with the help they need. For instance, it is cheaper to provide a wheelchair and make a house wheelchair accessible than it is to place someone into a facility, but then there are other needs to be met.

The PACE staff learns the needs of individuals and provides things such as modifications to bathrooms, assistance with diet planning, meal preparation, transportation, prescription drug management, nursing, respite for caregivers, and other aspects of home care. Nurses made home visits and coached caregivers.

The PACE team was able to visit and check on participants on a regular basis. Early detection of ailments is key to reducing the costs of health care, but when a doctor only sees a patient once a year, if that often, then illnesses can turn serious and costly. Everyone from the van driver to the director noted changes in a participant's behavior, appearance or other indicators and notified the team to check on the participant. So much of care is being aware.

The PACE staff inspected our house for safety concerns and gave Carol a physical checkup. A mental health specialist came to the house and gave Carol a series of tests, including a mental evaluation. Carol was accepted into the PACE program in September of 2008, the second month it was open for business.

The term "All Inclusive" meant all of Carol's care including medical services, doctors, dental and vision services, medicines, and medical equipment were covered. The care is more holistic than just medical care. If I couldn't drive Carol to doctors and other necessary places, PACE provided transportation. A van picked her up on weekdays and took her to the SCC for day care. The fully staffed center had a doctor, registered nurses, occupational and physical therapists, activities director, social workers, and support staff. The center furnished a lunch, snacks, exercise equipment, a piano, and even a pool table. An onsite beautician lifted the spirits of the ladies.

Carol was soon going on field trips to the botanical garden, viewing the aspen color change, shopping, and some of the men even went fishing. At the center Carol was creating seasonal greeting cards and crafts, singing songs, playing Bingo and other games, watching movies on a wide screen TV, and she did get upset if she didn't get her fifteen minutes on the exercise cycle. They celebrated birthdays, had special dinners for families, and activities galore. A quiet room with a bed was available when needed. Participants and their caregivers alike looked forward to going to a happy place. I believe the staff also looked forward to working in such a positive environment. For some participants such as Carol, her nearly five happy years at the SCC were transitional to moving into a skilled nursing facility.

Carol was reluctant to go to PACE at first unless she could take our little dog Muffin. Since the facility was pet friendly, Muffin got to go and she enjoyed all the attention and made a lot of people smile. When Carol started with PACE her gait was a shuffle and she was falling. We were afraid a fall would be serious, but within a couple weeks the Occupational Therapist had her walking smartly and restored her balance. Carol had the will to get better.

Then one morning Carol announced she didn't want to take Muffin anymore, because she was too busy and Muffin was getting in the way. It only took a couple weeks and she was looking forward to going to the center. She got herself dressed and ready for the day and was often looking out the window for the arrival of the PACE van. She had something positive to look forward to every week day.

When anyone enters the building it becomes obvious from the friendly and helpful demeanor of the receptionist that this is a happy place to work.

It is reflected back with participant's happy faces. The atmosphere is so positive. Cost-benefit ratios are one thing, but they cannot measure the positive physical and mental impacts generated by the feelings of a participant and his or her caregiver.

One day Carol told a nurse she didn't feel well. The nurse took her vital signs and discovered her blood pressure was dangerously high. The nurse called me and having conferred with a doctor called for an ambulance. Due to early detection PACE took her to the hospital ER and she was admitted for treatment for high blood pressure and soon released. The doctor prescribed proper medications to control her blood pressure and she has done well under his care. Carol kept all her doctors, but through PACE each physician knew what the others were prescribing and could take into consideration all of her medical issues.

Carol was still having problems remembering who I was all the time. I knew other caregivers who had experienced the painful feeling that their loved one no longer recognized them. I wasn't devastated, but the realization that the disease was progressing into another phase became very real to me. I could only stay in denial for so long. It's like a toothache - pretty soon you can't deny the increasing pain and have to do something about it.

Carol was soon one of the veteran participants and having been a school teacher, she wanted to help. The center got an old popcorn popper and Carol was the "popcorn girl" who handed out little bags of popcorn to any takers. One day I was feeling sick and Carol told me she would stay home and take care of me, but she had a job and they were depending on her. Staff looked all the time for things to give participants a sense of being needed and doing something for others. Morale of participants and the staff was high. The staff was rewarded by being a part of people's lives and seeing them respond to therapy, social interaction, and belonging to an extended family.

The care was very personal. There were a lot of hugs. Some participants came because of physical impairments and others with dementia. As caregivers we were perhaps the greatest beneficiaries of PACE. We appreciated the professional care. Sometimes the word "professional" has a connotation of being cold and uncaring, but our PACE staff set the standard for professional TLC. On the downside, staff people felt sadness and a real sense of loss when a participant died or had to leave for the services of a skilled nursing home. PACE and VOA (as well as most care facilities) placed a very high priority on regular in service training of their staffs. Good leadership is not satisfied with the status quo, but looks for innovation and implementing cutting edge technology and community servicing programs.

During regularly scheduled conferences with the staff, someone always asked how I was getting along. I don't know about women, but as a man it isn't manly for me to admit that I needed help. Watch out for male caregivers who say, "I'm fine." They are probably lying. If you are close to someone, you might pursue them with, "How are you-really? And don't give me that fine stuff. This is your friend asking."

Tim never let me get by with, "Fine." He knew the truth about me and communicated to PACE that I needed some relief. As a result, the team recommended several times that we place Carol into respite care, not for her, but for me, to give me a break when I was suffering caregiver's burnout. Some respite was for a week so I could recuperate from the stress. I look back now and am amazed how taking care of myself made it possible for me to take care of Carol for nearly five years at home. Our doctor said if she wasn't in the PACE program she would have to be in a skilled nursing facility.

As a caregiver, my anxiety went way down. I got off the anti-depressant. I had time for myself without being consumed with responsibility for those few hours each day. Every afternoon the driver brought Carol home at 3:30 sharp. PACE contracted with a home care business to provide a home care specialist two days a week for two hours to help me with light housekeeping and cooked our supper. I must admit I got a little spoiled. I was a good cook over a campfire, but kitchen duty was not my cup of tea. Once in a while I needed someone to be with Carol when I had a meeting and if I couldn't get someone from my family or church family to sit with her, PACE provided a caregiver for a few hours.

A representative from the national PACE program from Baltimore, Maryland interviewed us. He wanted to meet some of the people in the program rather than just reading statistics, reports, and evaluations. At that time Montrose PACE was a pilot program and under scrutiny. It was the first and is still the only rural PACE center in Colorado at this time (2015).

During the interview he asked Carol, "What have you gotten out of PACE?" Unprompted and without hesitation Carol answered, "I got my life back!" He had that "WOW-AWESOME" look on his face. He asked me if I had given up anything and I answered, "I've lost a load of stress and anxiety." Life had smoothed out, but the trail ahead would be fraught with pain and uncertainty. Perhaps you understand why I am such a supporter and cheerleader for such a successful program.

CHAPTER 6

Coping the Best I Can
(Cranking along without getting too cranky)

When I placed Carol into the PACE program I soon felt the peace that we were where God wanted us to be. I had full confidence when she was at the PACE center she was in good hands. I was more relaxed and life had leveled. Carol was a real blessing to those staff members who looked after her. They were excited about how well Carol did and I was glad to hear that she responded to their care.

However, it wasn't long until the rest of the story wasn't all that rosy. I was back on the roller coaster. Before long the stress during the evenings and weekends continued to weigh heavier on me. On weekends I came to the point that I couldn't wait for 8:30 Monday morning when the PACE van would pick her up.

Carol was having bouts of anxiety depression. I didn't know whether I was dealing with depression or dementia and sometimes both at the same time. Then one day Carol told me she was having suicidal thoughts and asked me to remove my guns from the house. She wasn't planning suicide, but she considered it as an escape from the pain of her anxiety.

Carol was an accomplished seamstress and enjoyed sewing, but she forgot how to thread and insert needles into her sewing machine. She volunteered to quit sewing and gave up her passion for quilting. I was proud of her for showing some cognitive ability and judgement. But, she tried to put me on a guilt trip, because she had given up so much and thought I should give up the things I enjoyed so that I could take care of her. She was grieving the loss of things she enjoyed doing and wanted me to fill the void.

I tried to help by doing things we could enjoy together as much as possible. In the summer we took Jeep trips into the nearby San Juan Mountains. Getting into the mountains was therapeutic for both of us. We preferred bumpy Jeep roads in high country rather than wide open straight roads and flat land. I couldn't scare her when we came to dangerous stretches on the road. She loved to say, "You got three wheels on the ground . . . you can make it." She was a lot of fun.

We photographed the beautiful scenery, identified flowers and watched wild critters. We enjoyed picnics amongst beautiful natural flower gardens, in the shade of tall spruce trees next to a babbling creek, or sitting high on alpine tundra overlooking the valleys below. In the fall we drove back country roads through aspen forests with dazzling yellow, gold, and reddish-orange colors. The back country roads were snowbound in the winter, so we drove up to Ouray "The Switzerland of America." We often saw bighorn sheep, elk or deer along the way. We stood in the cold and watched sled dog races on Red Mountain Pass and the ice climbers at the Ouray Ice Park. Sometimes we just drove around the country side. A few times we took a dip in the Ouray Hot Springs Pool. We both just needed to get out and away.

I kept a journal and noted in most entries that Carol's memory was deteriorating and she was having anxiety attacks. I took particular note of the many times she admitted to me that her memory was failing and she couldn't remember where she put things or put things in the wrong places. The intensity of her paranoia began to increase and she began withdrawing, but I believe her time at the PACE center slowed the progress by engaging her verbally or with activities. She responded so well to the staff and activities.

At home however, she hid heirlooms, because she thought someone from her past was going to break into the house and steal them. She hid or threw away a pair of my hearing aids. I hope some things are still in the house and perhaps I'll find them someday.

I had heard and read about short and long term memory loss. Like most caregivers I had to listen to the constant repetition of the same question or making the same statement every few minutes until I changed the subject. I thought that was short term memory (which it is.) Carol could still remember rather clearly those things which had occurred decades before.

Then one day she asked me why we divorced and I told her we had never divorced and we were still married. Reasoning with her failed as usual. It wasn't until years later when it dawned on me that I had become part of her short term memory. We've been married twenty years and that is now short term. She remembered her first mother-in-law, but didn't remember my mother whom she had known more recently. Her first husband and I have the same first name and she tried to call him. Even though they had been divorced for several decades, he was one of those at home people she wanted to return to the happy and secure feelings and reminded her the happy and secure feelings of good days.

Carol gradually became disoriented as to time and space. She didn't know the seasons or where she was. She woke me up one night by turning on the light and telling me to get dressed, because we had to travel. She thought we were living in Texas and had to go someplace. She also thought we lived out in the country and had several houses. She woke me up another night to tell me a man was going to steal Muffin. Yet another man was going to steal an antique lamp. She thought three boys were living with us and kept wondering where they were. These scenarios all happened within a couple days. I wrote in my journal: "This is all becoming very frustrating to me. At times I feel like throwing up my hands and just give up trying to cope with her dementia and yet I will not abandon her. She needs me more than ever."

Carol's physical health was pretty good, but one afternoon I found her asleep in her recliner and noticed she wasn't breathing well. Having been an EMT, I took her pulse and it was very weak and her breathing very shallow. She looked like she was in shock to me.

I called her name to wake her up and got no response. I called louder and rubbed her arm. Still no response. I pinched her skin and gently shook her. I called 911. A police officer responded immediately and EMTs arrived just as she regained consciousness. They gave her oxygen and took her vitals. She was breathing okay and her pulse was strong. I was pleasantly surprised when an EMT asked her name and who I was. She remembered. Although she seemed okay, the EMTs and I felt she should be transported to the hospital in case she had a stroke. The hospital staff tested and checked her out and we never did discover what caused her to be unconscious and unresponsive.

A few days later, Carol refused to go to church because she thought her ex-husband and his wife had a key to the house and were going to break in and steal things. She put out four bowls of cat food, because she thought we had four cats (we had two). I just left the bowls where they were. I took her for a drive and we had a picnic lunch under the pine tree where we were married. I thought romancing her might help. Instead, she got mad and accused me of running off with another woman and I had deserted her and was trying to get back into her graces. I was disappointed. The day went sour, but I understood what was happening. I had learned to accept her rejection with grace. She said, "Take me home."

Every caregiver website, conference, and book I ever checked out stressed the need to "Take good care of yourself." How can you take care of someone else if you don't take care of yourself first? Well, that's easier said than done. It's sort of like the old saying, "It's hard to concentrate on draining the swamp when you are up to your hip pockets in alligators." Stress, like an alligator, was eating me up. I wasn't very good at taking care of myself for years and I paid the price. I found I just didn't accidently do something for myself. I had to plan ahead. Again, easier said than done.

A good question we sometimes ask in a support group is, "What is something you've always wanted to do and never did or something you'd like to do again?" Make a plan and do it. A few years ago I decided I was getting old enough that I didn't have many years left that I could hunt elk. Hunting has been a major part of my life and I had given up part of me. For those who have never hunted, the killing of an elk or any animal is actually anticlimactic to the hunting experience. I cherish the memories I have had hunting with my dad, friends, and my son Ralph.

I had been saving up preference points and finally drew an elk license in 2007 for my old stomping grounds in the Upper Rio Grande in Southwestern Colorado. By then however, Carol's dementia was dominating our lives. I had waited six years and finally drew a license, but I couldn't leave her alone for most of a week and ask someone to come to the house. I could have asked for some respite care, but Carol was begging to go to hunting camp with me. Her enmeshment was destroying my dream hunt.

I knew I would have to have help in case I was successful, because I had lost so much strength and stamina due to Myasthenia gravis. I shared this with my close friend Larry, a retired Texas Game Warden who has been like a brother to me. We had shared many outdoor adventures and even though he couldn't hunt, he volunteered to come up from Crowley, Texas and help me. In addition, his wife Donna volunteered to come along just to be with Carol. Some other friends of mine gave us the use of their cabin in the middle of the hunting area, so we made plans.

I was excited. In my dreams I planned where the elk would be opening morning and I'd be in one of my favorite spots when my big bull walked out in front of me. Any elk hunter reading this is thinking "Yeah right."

Carol had some anxiety about the trip, but when it came to the day we drove to camp she seemed ready for the adventure. It was early October when the temperature drops below freezing at night and the air is crisp all day long. We got to hunting camp a couple days early to fire up the wood burning stove and get the cabin warm. When Larry and Donna arrived we were rewarded by sight of a moose walking slowly past the cabin, and a herd of Rocky Mountain bighorn sheep were grazing in the cliffs above us. Ducks and geese were enjoying the solitude of the lake fifty yards from the cabin. The elk must have known hunting season was upon them and they were hiding. It doesn't get any better than this. Carol's anxiety diminished and hallucinations stopped during the hunt. Donna spent time with her and they shared some 'girl' talk while Larry and I were scouting.

Opening morning Larry drove me to my spot. I hiked a short distance and waited for daylight. Through the dim light of dawn I could see my bull elk was not where he were supposed to be. Then God, having a sense of humor, sent a snow squall up the draw and I was in a whiteout for an hour. No elk opening morning. It snowed off and on all week, which made for good hunting conditions. The fellowship was rich and Carol was not having hallucinations or anxiety. She enjoyed Donna's company.

The log cabin was warm and cozy even when a frigid snow squall blew down the valley. We kept the fire burning. Finally on the last day and with a half hour of sunshine remaining, we spotted a small elk herd. I shot and killed a large bull elk. Larry and I boned out nearly two-hundred pounds of elk meat. We, our friends, and family ate elk meat all winter. I didn't have to kill an elk to have a great hunt, but being out in the San Juan high country with friends and making memories were the most important to me. I have a set of antlers on the wall next to the fireplace to remind me of my last hunt.

Carol enjoyed the experience of a hunting camp with good friends. It was the last time we were able to be away in wild country together. I will never forget that trip, but now Carol looks at the pictures and doesn't remember anything about it. Nevertheless, I learned to grasp the moment and enjoy what I could, and be thankful. In the fifteen years that I've been Carol's caregiver, this was the highlight example of taking care of myself.

Being good to yourself doesn't require grandiose plans to exotic places. Some just want some quiet time for a few hours several times a week, or go shopping or out to eat with some friends. One of the biggest obstacles for caregivers of loved ones with dementia is the fear of leaving him or her alone for even a brief time. Yet, asking someone to sit with a dementia patient who doesn't understand the basics of care can be a set up for disaster.

Soon after we returned from our hunting trip life returned to normal. I took care of Carol, went to work three days a week, to church, and shopping. Going to Walmart and City Market were my social opportunities when I might see someone I knew who had a few minutes to visit. I was back to not taking care of myself and my health was going downhill. I had the typical burnout symptoms of sleepless nights, depression, and dealing with all the ramifications of dementia.

A 1999 study reported in the Journal of the American Medical Association found elderly spousal caregivers (ages 66 to 96) who experienced caregiving-related stress have a 63% higher mortality rate than non-caregiving peers of the same sage. That statistic should motivate caregivers to pay attention to their own health.

In the spring of 2008 I developed a scratchy throat and within thirty-six hours I was coughing up blood. I told Carol to call 911. An ambulance crew transported me to the hospital. Some vicious little bacteria got into my lungs and caused pneumonia and then a pulmonary embolism. I was in ICU for five days, but obviously survived. During that episode Carol was home alone much of the time. I was unable to look after her, but all time she knew who I was and was able to find her way to the hospital. Perhaps the stress of being my caregiver helped her concentrate and focus. When she came to see me, I could tell she was struggling with who, what, when and where.

I was beginning to accept the reality that I was going to have an uphill battle to regain my strength to take care of myself and Carol. Over a period of time married people experience being short term caregivers for each other to get through illnesses and injuries, but long term caregiving is a different ball game. Long term caregiving tests the metal and bonds of a marriage. It either strengthens a relationship or the bond breaks.

Carol had periodic memory lapses about who I was since 2005 and by 2009 she didn't know who I was most of the time. Soon after my bout with pneumonia she called Ralph and asked, "Who is the man in my house?" Ralph explained, "That is my dad and your husband Glen." It's interesting that she always knew Ralph, but not me. She began to be very afraid of me. Several times Tim came to the house to convince her that I was her husband. Sometimes, the only progress he made was to convince her that he knew me and she was safe being in the house with me. She reluctantly trusted him. This was the beginning of my periodically sleeping in the guest bedroom.

I started this book with the story about Carol calling 911 to have me arrested as the strange man in her bed. Police responded two more times to have me arrested because she didn't know me. The valley of depression was becoming a box canyon that was getting deeper and darker every day and the trail becoming obscure.

I pause here to pay tribute to our Montrose City Police Department. Our 911 operators and the officers who responded to our calls were most professional and having been in law enforcement myself, I was aware of how they implemented their *Verbal Judo* training to handle such delicate situations. They use this training to reduce the emotional threat level in situations that can become violent. The same principles applied to help Carol. Our officers were compassionate beyond their paychecks and dedication that defined the logo *"To Serve and Protect"* written on the sides of their police cars. In every case they were able to calm her down to the point where she would at least let me sleep in the guest bedroom.

By the next morning however, she asked me why I was sleeping in the guest bedroom instead of with her. She had no memory of the incident and felt badly. I comforted her and assured her of my love and I looked forward to her coming home from PACE. She went to PACE and did fine, but when the van driver brought her home, she began to refuse to come into the house, because I was at the door waiting. The van driver had to convince her that it was safe for her to come into the house with me. She was reluctant, but went inside. This became a common occurrence.

Carol began wandering around the house looking into each room and she seemed lost. Then she started wandering out of the house. I bought some alarms at a local hardware store and installed them on the doors to alert me if she left while I was home.

The Montrose County Sheriff's Department provided a radio transmitter bracelet, so they could locate her if she wandered very far from the house. I was afraid of leaving her at home for any length of time at all. If I went to the store only three blocks away, she might not be home when I returned.

Once she went out the door into the back yard, through a gate, and up the street. An alert neighbor knocked on the front door and told me Carol was walking up the street. I called the police and an officer and our neighbor brought her back to his house across the street, because she wouldn't come into our house. I called Ralph on my cell phone and even her son who lived in North Carolina to talk to her and they tried to convince her that it was safe and she wouldn't budge. I left the house and the officer was able to escort her into the house. The perseverance of the officer's calming influence and authority finally settled her down to where she let me walk back into the house and to the guest bedroom. I was getting to be on a first name basis with the 911 operator and several officers. There are advantages to small town life.

I started wondering for how long I could go on. I started thinking about my future. There was a temptation to become a victim by thinking and living "this isn't fair. This isn't what I had in mind for retirement. What's going to happen to me?" Dementia patients often live more than twenty years with the disease. I don't want to lose Carol, because I love her so much, but what kind of a life is she going to have? I knew from my experience with my mother's disease what was ahead, but dealing with a parent is far different than taking care of a spouse.

The message came back to my mind, "All things work together for good. . ." Yes, Lord, I know, but right now I'm having a problem seeing good in this. An answer came into my heart of hearts "Trust Me." I responded, "Lord, grant me patience and please be quick about it." God's kind of patience however, doesn't come in a cup, but is a lasting gift to believers. Our issue is that we tend to leave God out of our thinking and miss the peace that surpasses understanding. The "good" was yet to come and it has in many ways, but it took time.

I had regular conferences with PACE as Carol's condition deteriorated. I began sending email messages to her social worker to keep him advised about what was going on at home. It was very important for him to know and to keep the PACE team advised. I also kept Tim, her neurologist, psychiatrist, and family doctor advised. I knew that when the time came to place her into a facility our entire team had to be on the same page.

I've attended several workshops sponsored by the Alzheimer's Association. The workshops, publications, and support for caregivers is something every new caregiver should take advantage of. The Association stresses the importance of building a support team including doctors, counselors, family, social workers and anyone else who is involved. Informed caregivers avoid being blindsided with responsibilities and decisions they didn't see coming.

One of the greatest highlights during this time came when PACE brought Naomi Feil to Montrose for a caregiver seminar. I describe this amazing lady as the International Caregiver's Guru. She has published several outstanding books such as *Validation: Techniques for Dementia Care: The Family Guide to Improving Communication* authored by Vicki de Klerk-Rubin. I will not go into detail about the seminar or Naomi's credentials, which are substantial, but I put her training to the test. The Validation technique of communicating with Carol helped me survive the next few years. It's one of the best, but not the only tool in my caregiver's toolbox.

I wrote earlier about Carol walking into the living room and asking me if I saw a black dog. After going through Validation training I avoided the reality approach and instead I used a Validation technique. I laid aside my reality and focused on her feelings. The long term memory of that dog evoked pleasant memories.

When it happened again I said, "You really loved that dog don't you?" She answered, "Yes." "What's his name?" I asked. She couldn't remember. I asked her if she loved to play with the dog and she smiled as she started telling me how she put dresses on him. She was remembering happier times with her dog and the pleasant feelings of their companionship.

I assured her that I'd look for him and I was sure he was safe. Her anxiety went down as did my own. I then redirected her attention to something else. I learned that attempting to bring her to reality was impossible, but respecting her feelings and meeting her where she was in her mind was a better place to start a conversation. My anxiety and blood pressure dropped, because there was no argument. Validation is an effective communication technique, but it takes more than one tool in a toolbox to get a job done.

One common scenario caregivers experience is when a loved one asks about a parent or loved one who has died. Carol often asked, "Where is mother?" I used to tell her she died, but Carol wouldn't accept that reality, because she had just talked to her or had seen her. Reality therapy got me nowhere.

Rather than tell Carol her mother died two decades ago, I found a "memory trigger" that worked for several years. Based on what she had told me about her mother (who died of AD), I asked her about the last time she saw her mother (in a casket.) She couldn't remember. I said to her, "You told me once that you bought her a beautiful blue dress. Tell me about that dress." Bingo! Carol said, "I bought the dress to have her buried in." She was able to process what she had just said and she concluded, "Mother is dead isn't she?" I put my arm around her and held her. Then I'd validate her feelings, by saying, "You really loved your mother didn't you?" She continued to have this same confusion or hallucination.

There is a difference between agreeing and validating. Sometimes a person just has to dump the painful memories and those are showered on the caregiver. Sometimes a caregiver needs to be more like a raincoat shedding pain and not be a sponge, soaking up a loved one's grief. Some patients can handle the truth directly and others will begin sobbing, so no one approach fits all. I believe when a loved one hallucinates about a person or object, they may really be thinking about the feelings that person or object gave them. I learned to concentrate on those feelings.

For some time Carol carried her big purse everywhere she went. It gave her a sense of owning something and a status more important than what was in it. One time I told her she didn't need a purse anymore. That was the wrong thing to say, because to her a purse was a part who she thinks she is.

I've found keeping a journal has been cathartic and helpful. Here are some out-of-context familiar reactions that I wrote in my journal that will resound with caregivers:

"I've started closing conversations that are going sour."

"I feel like I am living in a blender,"

"I'm having more anxiety all the time trying to get through the day."

"At times I just have to get up and go spend a few minutes by myself and refocus."

"So many hallucinations today that I couldn't keep track of them."

"Carol wants a divorce because she thinks I want to buy an airplane."

"Had to sleep in the guest bed, because Glen [that's me] would come home and catch us in bed."

"It is really dragging me down to come home to such a negative environment."

"If I speak to a woman, she thinks I'm committing adultery."

"There is more than I can write but it started getting to me."

"Couldn't sleep because she kept asking me questions and had to go to the guest bed."

"Praying with Carol quiets her spirit."

"I couldn't go to church because she was having suicidal thoughts and I didn't dare leave her alone."

"I feel like I'm on an unending roller coaster with so many ups and downs and sharp curves."

"I feel like I'm at the end of my rope."

I had another shocker one evening while we were watching television. Carol turned to me and asked, "Who are you?" I had been dealing with her not knowing who I was, but the outcome of this question floored me. I answered with a question, "Who do you think I am?" She answered, "You're my daddy!" I told her I was her husband. I showed her my driver's license, I showed her our marriage license, pictures of our wedding and nothing I produced convinced her otherwise. I asked her how old her daddy would be and she thought awhile and said about nighty-five years old. I asked her if she thought I looked that old and she looked me over and said, "No" and dropped the subject.

I told Tim and at the next counseling session he asked Carol, "Who is that man sitting next to you?" She answered, "That's my daddy." Being very insightful, Tim asked her, "If there was one thing you could have from your daddy, what would that be?" Without hesitation she answered, "His love." (Remember, her folks divorced when she was five years old). He continued, and if there is one thing you could give your daddy what would it be?" She answered, "I would give him my love." The last memory Carol had of her daddy was when she was on an elementary school field trip to a local bakery and saw her daddy working as a baker in front of a large oven during the war years. She knew in her heart that he loved her and she did have a couple pictures of him holding her when she was a little girl.

That evening we were again watching television and she turned to me and asked, "Who are you?" Here we go again. I again asked, "Who do you think I am?" She answered, "You're my daddy." I responded, "Well, come over here and sit on my lap." She sat on my lap and what she was really after was the love of her father, so I held her and loved on her. She needed to be cuddled, hugged, kissed, and hear and feel the words, "I love you." She returned my affection. She was so happy. Interestingly, the issue of my being her daddy never came up again.

Even though we were living in our house, she began asking, "Take me home." At first it was a house and all her clothes were in "that house." I asked her to describe the house and she described a house. Then, she said, "Let's go!" So I put her in the car and we started driving around town. I kept praying, "Please Lord, don't let us find a house that fits her description." I could just imagine her saying "That's it!" and wanting to go into the house and raid the closets for her clothes.

I realized it wasn't about a house, it was about clothes, dogs and cats and the feelings they gave her. She hallucinated that we had another house where we kept a menagerie of dogs and cats. She feared they hadn't been fed or watered and we had to find them. This time the search took us out into the farmlands of the county. We even drove into a farmer's yard, but his dog was a bit unfriendly, so we left. By the time we got back to town, she had forgotten why were out driving in the countryside.

She was disoriented to where we lived in Colorado. She kept thinking we were in Ada, Oklahoma where she was born and raised. I drove past the high school and asked her to read the signs and she read, "Montrose High School, Montrose Bank, Montrose City Limits, etc." She still thought we were in Ada, Oklahoma and couldn't understand why all the "Montrose" signs.

Even though she had lived in Texas most of her adult life, her memories were rooted in the earlier years in Oklahoma. Her mother is buried there. I drove a lot of miles trying to prove to her that she was hallucinating about houses. Driving her around was the same as trying to reason with her. It got me nowhere and frustrated her. At one point she accused me of deceiving her, because I didn't want her to find the house.

It has been years until it dawned on me; home was not necessarily a house or even a place, but were feelings about clothes, pets, her mother, children, among many other things I was unaware of. She wanted the security of her mother, even though she was very abusive. She wanted to mother her children who were young teenagers when she lost contact with them. I would continue to learn more about 'home.'

Carol grew up poor at the end of the Depression and as a little girl wore ragged clothes. So when she had the income, she began hoarding clothes and they gave her a sense of importance and value, of being good to herself. Carol was a cat lover and always had two cats close to her. Driving her around seeking to find non-existent houses and pets only exacerbated her anxiety and symptoms of dementia. These trips were counter-productive and gave her feelings of failure and great sadness.

CHAPTER 7

It's Time

My health took several big hits in 2011. My lifestyle, diet, along with years of stress contributed to needing four surgeries in March, June, July, and September. During those times when I was in and out of the hospital, PACE provided Carol with respite care. I learned during those periods how bad of shape I was in from the stress of being a caregiver. The reality really hit me that I wasn't as strong as my ego led me to believe. If I died, what would happen to Carol? I did all the planning through my will for finances, but there is more to taking care of her than just managing money.

My last surgery was for an abdominal abscess. It took me two months in the hospital and rehabilitation in Valley Manor and a full nine months for recovery. I was in horrendous pain and in serious condition. More than once I knew I was at death's door. My mind was often on Carol and I couldn't do anything but trust other people to take care of her. Some staff from PACE came by to check on me and asked what they could do for me, not just Carol. They truly cared for me, beyond their paychecks and job descriptions.

The word got around the prayer chain to pray for us. Donna, a deacon, contacted me and asked how they could help. She was my liaison with our church congregation. I gave her my daughter Lois' phone number. She called Lois and asked if there was any way she could help. Lois lived and worked about thirty miles away and said she needed to have someone go shopping for a new mattress for the guest bed, because one of our cats had ruined it. Later in the day she called Lois and reported that there was a new mattress and box springs on the bed. It was made and ready. Lois said to send her the bill, but Donna said she didn't know who replaced the bed and there was no bill.

Donna took Muffin to visit Carol and several times brought Carol to my hospital room. This experience taught me how precious support is and may be in part, the reason I am such an advocate for support groups. I had always been able to be on the giving end, but I was very humbled to be on the receiving end. Being humbled is good for the soul.

After a close brush with death, I was released from the Montrose Memorial Hospital to Valley Manor Rehabilitation Center. Carol lived in the memory care unit. We were able to spend time together and share meals while I was regaining my strength and healing. After I was discharged, I went home where Ralph and Lois cared for me until I could take care of myself.

In a couple weeks Carol came home and life with dementia started all over again. During her stay at Valley Manor we noticed she had settled into the structured environment, but when she came home the structure came down and old familiar symptoms of dementia kicked in. The structure involved the routine, familiar place, fewer decisions, socialization, medical checks and being cared for by the staff.

Carol went back to the PACE center for day care and some structure while she was there, but on the home front, life was going south. I couldn't replicate the structure she needed.

Carol called the police two more times to have me arrested, because I was a stranger in her house. The frequency and intensity of hallucinations were off the chart. She called 911 four times claiming I had kidnapped and was holding her against her will. I'm sure the emergency call center was concerned about dispatching an officer to respond to what must have sounded like the fable, *"The Boy Who Cried Wolf."*

It was a cold March morning in 2012. At two o'clock the phone rang. "This is the Montrose 911 operator calling. You need to talk to a policeman at your door." The adrenaline hit me and all I could think about were my kids and grandkids. I put my robe on and went to the door. I asked the officer what was going on and he answered, "It's about your wife." I told him I didn't understand, but I'd go get her. I thought she was in bed. Before I could turn around, he shocked me when he said, "No, she is five houses down the block!"

Without my knowing it, she got out of bed, slipped out of the house, and walked down the street in fifteen degree temperature, through the snow and ice, barefooted, and only wearing her nightgown. She could have fallen or died of hypothermia. Fortunately, when she got cold she rang a doorbell and a lady answered the door and had Carol come into her house. Carol didn't know her name or where she lived. The neighbor called 911. The responding officer knew Carol from previous calls he had made to the house. Another officer brought her home and I got her warmed up and back into bed.

Carol's walk down the street convinced me and everyone on our team that this behavior had become a serious danger. The next day I told Tim, our social worker, and our doctor what had happened. Our social worker passed the information on to the PACE team.

A couple days later I was in a counseling session and Carol was at the Senior Care Center. I was going out of my mind about what to do. My heart said to trust God, but I had to make decisions and I didn't know what to do next. Through all this I was slowly learning that God was using this circumstance to teach me to trust Him. When I carried the burden by myself it led to depression, and anxiety; however, when I focused on the fact that when I meditated and prayed for His will to be done, then I could relax and trust Him.

I prayed God's will be done and didn't instruct Him how I thought He should relieve my anxiety. In His perfect timing God answered my prayer. My cell phone rang. It wasn't God, but our social worker. He said Carol's doctors and the PACE team had conferred and agreed, "IT IS TIME." I knew what he meant. I asked him what the timetable was and he answered, "Thirty minutes." I didn't even have proper time to worry and fret over the decision anymore.

Isn't that just like God? Arlene's assurance came true again: "When the time comes, it [the decision] will fall into our laps." For years I had dreaded that moment and yet when it came, I can't describe the tsunami of relief that swept over me. It had been like one moment an anchor was dragging me down and then suddenly I was in a lifeboat floating above the turmoil. Thank you Lord! I have met other caregivers who have had similar "drop in my lap" experiences.

The PACE team transported Carol from the Senior Community Care Center directly to

Freedom Hall (memory care unit) at Valley Manor. Having been there for respite care, Carol was going to a familiar place and a greeted by a friendly and loving staff. The transition had to have been one of the smoothest on record.

I went home and gathered clothing and items she would need for the first few days. The staff suggested that I stay away for a while to let her settle in. This is generally good advice, but I told the Director of Social Services that Carol had a tremendous fear of being abandoned and the longer I stayed away the worse she might get. I did go see her about the third day and she was glad to see me, although I wasn't sure if she really knew who I was.

I used the time to gather myself together. It was a shock to have reached the point where I knew I didn't have to deal with the dementia on an hourly basis. There was a certain aura of finality, not as in death, but my caregiver role changed. I never felt one pang of guilt. Some caregivers fall into a pit of guilt when their loved one is placed into skilled nursing care, but I repeat, "I was lovingly responsible." This wasn't a selfish decision. Intellectually, I knew I had done the right thing, but emotionally I was still torn between sadness and relief.

It took a few nights to get used to sleeping alone and not being awakened all hours of the night.

Muffin seemed to miss Carol too. The first night I lifted Muffin up onto the bed and she snuggled up against Carol's pillow. Our little dog became my companion and little buddy. The loneliness had already set in. I missed sleeping with Carol. I missed hearing her breath and an occasional snore.

Once Carol settled into the structure of her new home, I began visiting her almost daily. At the end of nearly every visit was the plea, "Take me home." She would hold onto my arm until I pulled away. It was heart breaking for both of us.

Before long I did not dread going in to visit Carol. I dreaded the awful feeling of leaving her and feeling sympathy for her feeling abandoned. I didn't want her having those feelings. I put myself in her shoes and how I would have hated to be left there. But, I can't put myself in her shoes-that's my reality.

Visiting Carol changed me. It took some time. At first I'd walk down the hall and look past all of the residents who were in wheel chairs and walkers. I didn't make eye contact with anyone. Muffin on the other hand, thought everyone who made eye contact wanted to pet her. I slowed down and Muffin ran to anyone who would pet her. I picked her up to let some of the wheelchair-bound residents love on her. Muffin reminded some residents of their pets. Just touching and petting a lively little dog lifted their spirits. One lady latched onto Muffin and it took two nurses to pry her grip off "MY DOG!" I learned to be more careful.

I was visiting Carol one day when Mary came into the room in her wheel chair. She looked up on the wall and saw a picture of Carol and me. She said, "I want my picture." Rather than explain the picture was of Carol and me, I asked her, "Who is in that picture?" She answered it was a picture of her and her husband. Rather than reason with her I said, "You must really love him." She replied how she loved and missed him. She shared some memories of him.

I asked her if she liked dogs. When she answered "yes," I asked her if she would like to pet my dog. I held Muffin up to her and she began petting my little fur ball. As she stroked Muffin she smiled. I complimented her and said, "Oh Mary, you have such a beautiful smile. I hope the next time I come visit my wife you'll give me a big smile." Later when I went into Freedom Hall, I made a point to see Mary and when she saw Muffin and me she always smiled. I wanted to be a blessing to Mary and without her being aware, she was a blessing to me.

At first I took Carol off the unit once a week for a drive into the nearby San Juan Mountains. We'd stop and get a Coke, with ice (inside joke). I was able to get her mind away from the nursing home and there was always something for her to see.

However, as time went on I learned that the longer we stayed away, the more likely she would start becoming disoriented and incontinent. We started taking shorter trips and before long I could take her on the same nearby road time after time and she'd say, "I've never been on this road before." We enjoyed the same beautiful scenery many times.

On the way back to Valley Manor we stopped by the Cold Stone Creamery for her favorite sundae and spent some time in our house. At first she knew where she was, but then one day she was wandering up and down the hallway and asked, "Where are the stairs to the basement?" I told her this house didn't have a basement. She wandered through the house and I could tell she didn't realize she was at home. After I took her back to Valley Manor, she asked me, "Where do you live?" I answered that I lived in a house about a mile away. I quit using the word 'home.' Carol only occasionally realized I was her husband. She knew my name, but told others I was her friend. She was becoming so incontinent and I couldn't take her out anymore. In time she adjusted to not going on drives into the mountains.

Carol started calling me from the nursing home and ordering me to "Take me home." I asked the staff to not call me and hand her the phone anymore. She had called directory assistance and asked for the phone numbers of her late uncle, father, step father, and her mother who were all buried in Oklahoma. I believe she was seeking people from her past who gave her love, security, and a sense of well-being. She was desperate to get in contact in any way she could. She wanted to return to her roots.

She thought her car was parked outside and she could still drive home. The staff did their best to get her mind off of going home by encouraging her to participate in activities. None of us fully understood the meaning of her wanting to reconnect and the importance of her feelings.

Being disoriented is like being adrift in a sailboat with no compass on a cloudy, windless day out in the ocean and no idea where land is. You want to get to land, but have no idea which way to go or how you'd get there. It was difficult to help Carol when she asked, "Where am I?" I kept my answer concise, "Montrose, Colorado." That was too much information for her to process. Because she didn't know where she was, she was surprised I knew where she lived. She usually asked, "How did you find me?" I touched her and said, "This is your home and where you live and I always know where you are and I am here to visit you." She seemed satisfied, but then she kept repeating the question until I redirected the conversation.

One day Carol was standing by the locked door when I walked in. I asked her where she was going and she said she was going to walk across the street to the train tracks and catch a train back home to Ada [Oklahoma]. When she was a little girl the first house she lived in was down near the railroad tracks at the edge of town. Sometimes she thought I lived in Ada and drove all the way to Colorado to be with her. I never corrected her perception. It didn't matter where I came from.

I started participating in two caregiver support groups and one online support website. These support groups were smaller and more intimate than the one I attended when I was taking care of my mother. These were more like walking into a wilderness camp and being with fellow sojourners. My role amongst these folks was more of the veteran sharing and reaching out to folks who were new to their role as caregivers. The people who came were at various stages of caregiving.

Newcomers to caregiving immediately gained support to help them grasp onto the need to educate themselves by attending workshops, seminars, and taking advantage of the Alzheimer's Association's programs to get started. You can read all the material that has been written, but having a mentor or association with folks in a support group over time does more to help a new caregiver. Some people naturally felt trapped with no way out, but being with total strangers who have gone through similar circumstances lifted their spirits and refreshed their souls. Newcomers were assured that what was said in the room stayed in the room. After attending just a few meetings and asking lots of questions, newcomers experienced honest and caring folks, just like themselves. More than once I've seen a newcomer break down and cry and someone would speak up and say, "Six months ago I was sitting in your chair and crying too. I understand how you must be feeling." Sometimes there were reassuring hugs and everybody needs a hug now and then.

After sharing the common symptoms of 'caregiver burnout' someone asked, "Does your doctor know about your sleeplessness, fatigue, anxiety, and physical ailments?" Caregivers often ignore their own symptoms, because the focus is on their loved one. Down the road it is very important for the doctor to know the needs of the caregiver, so health issues can be addressed before they become serious. I didn't do this until I got so sick I couldn't deny my health issues any longer.

We men are probably more prone to hide the truth, because we were taught, "Big boys don't cry." Any admission to a weakness is a blow to our fragile egos and we cover up by saying, "I'm fine." I had a good friend ask me how I was doing. I told him, "Fine." He looked me straight in the eye and said, "You're lying through your teeth!" He saw right through my façade. I love him for teaching me it was safe to share my pain without it being a "pity party." Sometimes the pain and sense of hopelessness drives us to seek help. I'm glad my circumstances drove me to seek help to take care of Carol. I wish I hadn't waited so long.

In our support groups we shared things that worked and sometimes our efforts seemed to fail. We laughed and cried together. Our groups were usually less than ten people and is a good sized group for sharing things that are close to the heart. Larger groups offer more opportunity for guest speakers and programs that are educational. There is a need for both.

In our area, Region 10, is also the Agency on Aging and Disability Resource Center. It provides assistance for the elderly and for those who take care of them. Besides connecting caregivers to local resources and programs for direct, Region 10 sponsors an annual Caregiver Summit. Many caregivers would love to attend such events, but can't or don't want to leave their loved one alone. So Region 10 pulls professional caregiver volunteers from nursing homes and home care providers to be with those that are homebound. Those who are ambulatory come to the Summit and volunteers provide them with activities, music, attention, and lunch while the caregiver attends the presentations and workshops. Nationally known speakers who are experts in the art and craft of caregiving, give presentations and lead workshops offering practical training for the many aspects of caregiving. Vendors present their company's goods and services that are available to caregivers. Overall, the Summit has been a successful outreach to caregivers.

CHAPTER 8

Living Outside the Box

People have asked me if my wife has Alzheimer's yet. In order to understand some things we put labels on people with certain symptoms and put them into boxes. Dementia is basically the failure of the brain to make the body perform its many tasks such as movement, speech, memory and all bodily functions. Dementia is not normal aging. According to experts (see Suggested Readings) there are dozens of causes and about seventy symptoms of dementia. Laura Wayman in her book *A Loving Approach to Dementia Care,* wrote that dementia is not a diagnosis, but a list of symptoms. According to her, Alzheimer's is under the umbrella of dementia that deals with memory loss and which is only diagnosed upon autopsy. Alzheimer's however, is a complex disease affecting not just memory, but the entire body. My purpose in even mentioning this is to avoid putting people into a labeled box. Regardless of whether the label or box says "Dementia" or "Alzheimer's," the issue is how to deal with these diseases in a loving and supportive way. The label doesn't matter one little bit.

My mother certainly had dementia but died of old age. My mom wasn't typical in many ways. She had several symptoms of dementia including memory loss. Unlike many patients however, in her later stages she knew my name and I was her son right up to near the end. On one of her annual visits Arlene introduced herself to mother, "I'm Arlene." Mother smiled and said, "I have a daughter named Arlene." She hadn't seen Arlene in a year, but soon knew who she was. I figure when you get to be ninety years old, you're entitled to get things mixed up now and then. Shucks, it happens even to teenagers, so what's the big deal?

When mother asked or demanded, "Take me home," she was thinking about the last house she lived in. However, what was it about living in her house that made her want to go back? It probably meant many things to her such as independence, security, sense of accomplishment, satisfaction, responsibility, spontaneity, control, and more than we can imagine, attached to the feelings of her house. In time she forgot what that house looked like and her plea was more, "Get me out of this place," which meant the nursing home. Yet, when I took her out for a drive or to our house, after a while she would say, "It's time to take me home now." So, home does not mean the same thing to everyone, but rather it has a dynamic meaning beyond what is in any dictionary.

Carol, on the other hand, home was the feelings of security, safety, and the love of her daddy, mother, stepfather, an aunt and uncle, a grandmother and they 'lived' in Oklahoma. She wanted to return to her roots. Even though Carol had an abusive mother, she was secure as a little girl and still felt responsibility for taking care of her. Carol's brain was still submissive to her dead mother's perfectionist demands. She reacted as she thought her mother would want her to respond.

Carol lost track of who I was during early onset. In some ways I was better off being her new friend with the same name as her first husband. She even asked me, "Which Glen are you"? I'd answer, "I'm the guy who loves you and comes to see you." When I was her friend she didn't demand, "Take me home." Rather than set her straight, I went along with being her friend and it sure made it a lot easier on me. At least she wasn't afraid of my being her friend.

One of the symptoms of dementia is called "sundowning." The demented person begins to wander in the late afternoon and into the night. One theory explains such behavior as being the result of the brain dying and wanting to resolve past relationships. For example, the brain may want to reconcile a long term broken relationship and so the behavior is explained, "I must go someplace and do something, but I don't know where or what I am supposed to do." Carol wandered out of the house once with clothes draped over her arm. I believe having nice clothes lifted her self-image and she was taking a change of clothes to wherever she was going. It really doesn't matter why, but how I dealt with her behavior that mattered.

Newcomers to our support groups introduce themselves and when they are comfortable they begin sharing a long list of frustrating behaviors and are uncertain how to handle them. Then someone asks, "How are you handling the situation or how does that make you feel about it?" I believe this question applies to all caregivers, not just those dealing with dementia. Sometimes it takes a couple sessions for a person to realize we are together to help each other cope with a loved one. How we feel about ourselves and how we handle situations is very important.

There is a big difference between being a home caregiver and a professional caregiver in a care facility. Today, there are facilities offering several options of care. For many years nursing homes were perceived as houses of gloom and doom. The media expounded stories of abuse, and mistreatment of residents. Although there are some horror stories about nursing homes, the fear and guilt of placing a loved one should not be a basis for such a serious decision. Some spouses and families have promised, "I will never put you in a nursing home." I had some of the same concerns. The stigma of past mistreatment continues. Government regulations changed some practices that needed changing and it was just good business for the industry itself to make positive changes beyond government edicts.

Although there are examples of mistreatment in nursing homes, consider the horror that some patients suffer in home settings. Some patients suffer benign neglect, mistreatment, inadequate medical attention, poor nutrition, inadequate exercise, and social interaction. I didn't neglect or mistreat Carol, but I couldn't get her to eat a balanced diet or to exercise. She had become a social recluse.

Loving family members may not understand what is happening to a loved one and to their changing relationship. There are loved ones who are so stubborn and will in no way cooperate. The family is trapped and even if they are unified, they are in a dilemma about what to do. When this happens it is time to seek professional counsel and build a support team. The Alzheimer's Association is a good place to start as well as local government assistance on aging.

As a caregiver I have witnessed major changes in nursing home care in the past thirty years. Please understand that my comments in no way disparages or is comparative to any such facilities nearby or far away. Consider also when one person may be totally pleased with the care given in a facility, others may not be not be at all satisfied. My experience has been limited to one skilled nursing care facility. My mother lived for nine years and Carol four years in Valley Manor Care Center in Montrose, Colorado. This facility is owned and operated by Volunteers of America (VOA) as a nonprofit corporation. When mother lived there, the facility was clean, the food had room for improvement, the ratio of staff to residents was barely acceptable, activities were adequate, the staff was dedicated, and I'd say the overall care was good. I never witnessed or even heard of any patient abuse.

Since Carol has been a resident, there have been several remodels of the campus, food service has greatly improved, the staff to resident ratio has improved, and the staff is more highly trained. It is my opinion, that the staff in any facility makes all the difference in care. A facility can have the best of amenities and landscaping, but it is the administration, nurses and staff who take care of the residents that make the difference between care that is acceptable or excellent. The common approach in most facilities up until recently was to use reality therapy to maintain and in some cases bring back residents to reality, which was usually a failure. There is currently a movement toward creating a more homey approach by more closely matching home life. Familiar music, decorations, pictures, table cloths, and other little things may serve as memory triggers and talking points about home.

Because time was important to me, I thought it was important to Carol, so I gave her a calendar to keep track of the days. In her shrinking world however, the day of the week was not important. I gave her a new watch, but she can't tell time. Carol complained that I never came to see her. I gave her a diary so she could write in it when I was there on a particular day. It made me feel better, but in reality it didn't work for her. She would look at it and still thought I never came to see her. It wasn't the day of the week or how long it was between visits. She was voicing her feelings of loneliness and being abandoned. At first I felt guilty that she didn't believe me, but in time I learned it wasn't about winning an argument or changing her. It was about loving her.

Shortly after Naomi Feil gave her workshop on Validation, several staff members attended her advanced training to become certified instructors. VOA took the lead in implementing the use of Validation as its approach for administering a new level of care. VOA trained nurses, CNAs, and other staff give more personal and intimate care to the individual residents. For example, rather than restrain a wanderer, a CNA would approach the individual and ask him where he was going. Depending on the response, the CNA would engage him by asking, "Who do you want to see? Tell me about that person, place, or thing. Where does he live? How do you get there?" Even if the resident is unable to express himself, he understands someone is listening to him. This has a calming effect and reduces inappropriate behavior.

I learned to ask: who, what, when, and where and avoid the "why" questions, because they often don't know why and not knowing may frustrate them even more. It would be far easier to avoid the contact and let the locked door do its job. However, the objective is to calm the person, not by restricting his movement or behavior, but by entering his world and bringing a sense of comfort and security.

The administration began a new weekly activity called 'group validation.' By getting to know more about each resident the leader took advantage of their abilities. Carol was a school teacher and she became the official greeter. Another lady led the singing and said a prayer. She had been a Sunday school teacher. Those residents who are alert enough to communicate, gather together and a trained staff member begins a conversation and encourages residents to share anything on their minds. It is interesting how they interact and even though they may not remember the facts of the conversation, they each leave with the good emotions. Some residents speak out who are mostly silent around others. As patients progress through the stages of dementia, they may have it together inside their brains, but have lost the ability to express themselves. How utterly frustrating it is to them. Through validation, caregivers can learn to communicate, not only in words, but in body language, touching, and even the use of music.

Being a home caregiver is a special gift from God. Yes, it's hard at times, but in the long run there is great reward; of being a faithful anchor to another person whom you love.

CHAPTER 9

I'm Going Home

I have watched Carol progress through the stages of dementia. Fifteen years ago she was in the early stage and able to walk, talk, laugh, and enjoy the big world around her. Her world has shrunk to a small room with a view of open space, but she doesn't see past the glass of her window. She sleeps much of the day and has to have assistance to dress, go to the bathroom or shower, and it takes two people to help her walk. She is beginning to use a wheelchair. She periodically falls. Her speech is often slurred, she speaks non words, and completing a sentence or thought escapes her mind. She is unaware of her surroundings. Yet, she can become very agitated by the slightest change. CNAs constantly monitor her vital signs. Although Carol never smoked, she has COPD and is on oxygen most of the time.

Although she is in late stage and her condition worsening, this could go on for a long time. I was faced with determining the level of care for end-of-life directives. This was a painful process subjecting myself to periods of the 'guilts' and wondering if I was doing the right thing for Carol. When it came down to signing a document that seemed like a death warrant, I knew I was making a commitment to end Carol's life down the road. "No CPR, no feeding tubes, no life sustaining equipment, no antibiotics except for some minor infection. . ." I approved comfort measures, pain relief, and oxygen. The document was not irrevocable, but with no propensity to improve, was basically set. I did this out of love. I reasoned there was no hope for restoration to a normal life and if emergency measures were taken to sustain her life, what kind of life would that be? We had talked about the issue soon after we were married and I knew how she felt. I don't want to prolong her agony. It is not irrational to be, "Lovingly responsible."

Across America there are six million people diagnosed with dementia/Alzheimer's and many caregivers who are on the front lines successfully fighting battles over dementia and other debilitating diseases, because they took advantage of community resources.

Some caregivers have not taken advantage of the resources available to them either because they haven't felt the need or are not aware of them. It is like going into battle with no plan for offense or defense, no training, no equipment, supplies, reinforcements, and no hope of sustainability for a long term victory. They are trapped just like I was until I sought help.

I believe the weak link in the caregiving process begins in the early stages when a caregiver becomes suspicious that something isn't quite right with a loved one. Normal aging happens and it is very easy to pass off forgetfulness and confusion. Early stage caregivers often spend time in denial until a behavior becomes dangerous or otherwise unacceptable. Often a caregiver gets to wits end and THEN will seek help. Some go to their family physician, a neurologist or a counselor to get a diagnosis. Some folks learn about our support group as their first attempt to seek help.

If a diagnosis of dementia is made, the support system in some communities leaves the caregiver to his or her own devices. Ideally what needs to happen is that a new caregiver comes alongside a mentor, be that through a local program, support group or other entity. Although they are helpful, it takes more than one session, attending a workshop, reading a book, or a basket full of brochures to provide the help a caregiver needs to begin this journey. A person needs more than information at this time. Even close friends who really care, but have no experience or perhaps bad experiences can leave a caregiver ill equipped to cope. Sometimes the best a friend can do is be a listener and not a 'fixer.' I had a friend comfort me by saying, "I have no idea of the pain you are having, but if you need someone to talk to please call upon me."

As the "Baby Boomers" age and dementia begins to inflict its terrifying sting into some of their lives, the burden of caring for them will fall onto the next generation. More needs to be done to educate future caregivers about the disease and the impact it is going to have on them. No matter what our health care system looks like, the sheer number of dementia cases that need care will overwhelm it.

As the American family unit continues to disintegrate, who will take responsibility for the care of loved and unlovable ones? I am concerned the present generation is affected by the political entitlement mentality and not taking responsibility for themselves and others. There is plenty of room in the back of our minds to live in fear of what might be. As a society I believe we need to be thinking outside the box of contemporary care and not be limited by status quo mindset.

Rather, I choose to look at the tremendous advances in professional caregiving and especially the empowerment of home caregivers to fill the gap. There is no silver bullet approach, but as a society, we must face the reality of dementia/AD as one of the major health concerns our nation faces. Researchers are working feverishly to find a cure, but we cannot sit back and wish this would happen and the problem go away.

My hope and faith has been in God. As I look back over the past thirty-five years of caregiving, I am amazed that I ever survived. I nearly died twice, but I believe the Lord had His purpose in allowing me to recover and take care of Carol. In addition, He changed my life and gave me a fresh and new purpose to be available to others who are struggling. I've been blessed by so many trailblazers and guideposts who have humbly reached out to me and kept me on the trail.

I hope that by sharing my journey it will encourage you to reach beyond yourself to others. As caregivers we need each other. No one else can understand what we are going through better than another caregiver. Be a trailblazer to someone else and remember those who have encouraged you in your time of need.

When my task is finished, I will not ask, "Take me home," but in God's time He will say to me, "It's Time. Come on Home."

In the meantime

HAPPY TRAILS TO YOU!

About the Author

Glen Hinshaw was born in 1941 and raised in Denver, Colorado. After graduating from North High School, he attended Colorado State University. He graduated in 1963 with a Bachelor of Science Degree in Wildlife Management. In his thirty-four year career with the Colorado Division of Parks and Wildlife he was a Wildlife Officer and retired as the Division's Regional Education Coordinator for Western Colorado.

Glen received awards for being "Wildlife Officer of the Year" in 1968, The Colorado Chapter of Trout Unlimited's "Conservationist of the Year" in 1985, "Most Positive Employee" award in 1989, and the "Enos Mills Lifetime Achievement Award for Environmental Education" in 1997.

After he retired in 1997 Glen wrote *Crusaders for Wildlife*, a 200 year history about wildlife stewardship in Southwestern Colorado. In 2014 he wrote his autobiography *Echoes from the Mountains: The Life and Adventures of a Colorado Wildlife Officer.*

For the past thirty-five years Glen has been a caregiver for his mother and wife who had dementia.

Suggested Reading and Resource List

A Loving Approach to Caregiving by Laura Wayman, published by John Hopkins University Press

Hope for the Caregiver by Peter Rosenberger, published by Worthy Inspired

The 36 Hour Day by Nancy Mace

Validation by Vicki de Klerk-Rubin R.N., M.B.A.
  (A whole series of books and DVDs)
These and many more books on caregiving for dementia patients are available on Amazon.com

Resources and Information:

The Alzheimer's Association, a major source of information

PACE   seniorcommunitycare.org

Local caregiver support groups

Local governmental resources for senior citizens

Caregiver websites

25050581R00081